We Love Each Other, But…

We Love Each Other, But...

A Leading Couples Therapist Shares the Simple Secrets That Will Help Save Your Relationship

Dr. Ellen Wachtel

Golden Books

New York

Golden Books®
888 Seventh Avenue
New York, NY 10106

Copyright © 1999 by Ellen Wachtel
All rights reserved, including the right of reproduction
in whole or in part in any form.
Golden Books® and colophon
are trademarks of Golden Books Publishing Co., Inc.

This book contains references to situations involving author's clients.
However, the names and other identifying characteristics have been changed
to protect the privacy of those involved.

Designed by Suzanne Noli

Manufactured in the United States of America

10 9 8 7 6 5 4 3 2 1

Library of Congress Cataloging-in-Publication Data

Wachtel, Ellen F.
    We love each other, but—: a leading couples therapist shares the simple
secrets that will help save your relationship / Ellen Wachtel.
        p.   cm.
    ISBN 1-58238-007-4 (alk. paper)
    1. Marriage—Psychological aspects   2. Marital conflict.   3. Com-
munication in marriage.   4. Marital psychotherapy.   I. Title.
HQ734.W14   1999
646.7′8—dc21   98-41337
                                                                          CIP

To my husband, Paul, and my
children, Kenneth and Karen. They are the bedrock on which
my life has been constructed. It is through
them that I learned how to love.

Contents

We Love Each Other, But . . .

Two summers ago my husband, Paul, and I found ourselves becoming friendly with a couple who, like us, were spending a week on Cape Cod in Massachusetts. After several mellow dinners together we drifted into a conversation about our marriages. I heard myself say that Paul and I are a lot alike and that's probably why, even though we met and married when we were quite young, our marriage of thirty years seems to be going along fairly well. Yet as the four of us started to compare likes and dislikes, it struck me that we were no more alike than our newfound friends. They talked of their many fundamental differences and the stress this placed on their relationship. As they ticked off their list—he's social, she's more of a loner, he's a sports-oriented person who loves outdoor activities while she is happiest staying at home, reading—I began to think about all the ways in which my husband and I differ. As with our new friends, many of our interests are not the same. My husband watches almost every Knicks game and is sometimes too excited to sleep after a good player trade, while watching more than ten minutes of a game puts me in a semistupor. I love in-line skating and ice-skating, and though

1

Paul sometimes joins me, as he puts it "balance is not my trump card." Poking around in flea markets is a real treat for me, but he becomes restless and agitated if he spends more than five minutes looking at what he calls junk.

We have more serious differences, too. I'm a planner, always thinking about the weeks, months, and even years ahead. My husband, on the other hand, finds a bit peculiar my wish for early-morning conversations about where we will live when we retire, or how often we will baby-sit for grandchildren, whom we are years away from having. When I worry about some possible problem that may or may not occur, he prefers not to talk or even think about it unless it actually happens. "Why worry about it now?" he asks, and I try once again to explain that I cope better if I'm prepared for the worst. We differ even on such fundamentals as child-rearing philosophies and religious convictions. Yet despite all of our differences, I genuinely do think of us as being basically alike.

The conversation that night sparked my wish to write this book. As we talked, I realized it wasn't that my husband and I were alike and the other couple were different. Instead it was that we tended to focus on our similarities while they emphasized their differences. Our friends politely disagreed with my point of view. "Aren't you just sweeping problems under the rug?" they suggested.

"No, I don't think so," I said. The wish to find common ground in a relationship has a profound effect on what happens between people. Emphasizing strengths and positives actually creates more and more positive interactions, so that the problems that have been overlooked become a less significant part of the relationship. The idea for this book began with my wish to explain exactly how this works.

• • •

So much of what I have learned in the twenty-five years I have worked with couples in marital therapy can be used by anyone willing to give a little thought and care to how he or she acts in a relationship. This book gives you some straightforward tips that will help you not only get along with your partner more smoothly but also preserve the warmth and intimacy that drew you together in the first place. I have found in my work with couples that often it is the basic, simple advice that seems to help most. Apologetically I find myself giving minilectures on how to act in a loving, supportive, and cooperative manner, and often couples tell me this grandmotherly advice has helped put their relationship back on-track.

This book will describe these simple, practical tips that hundreds of couples have found so useful. I have written it for all those—young and old, first-time marriage partners or repeaters (so to speak)—who question whether relationships can really thrive over long stretches of time. It will tell you not only how to maintain a good relationship over the course of many, many years but also how you can repair a relationship that seems to be going awry.

During the course of my career as a therapist I have worked with close to one thousand couples. Almost all of them started out together with love and high hopes, but by the time they came to see me many had reached the depths of despair. They had become disillusioned with their partner, with marriage, with love, and sometimes even with life. Adding to their misery was a sense of personal failure and confusing feelings of shame: shame for having made a poor choice in a partner, shame for remaining in a loveless marriage, shame for the ugliness of their arguments and who they have become, and even shame for being afraid to leave and go it alone.

How often I have heard people say that they once seemed so right for each other, so "in sync," and now all they seem to do is bicker and argue. Many of the couples I see in therapy feel that the person who seemed like she would be a best friend for life— maybe even a soul mate—now seems like someone with whom they have little in common. "We're so different from one another and just don't think the same way about things," is a common refrain from couples whose marriages are in trouble. "We hardly talk to each other anymore. What a disaster! It's so confusing. We thought we loved each other. Could it have been a mistake?"

Some Common Concerns

Many of the men and women who pass through my office are terribly worried that they no longer love their partner. They worry that they are bored, that they have grown and developed while their partner has remained in a rut. That they no longer find their partner interesting, exciting, or sexually attractive.

They worry because they don't really look forward to time alone with their partner, and after the kids are in bed they just want time to themselves. They wonder what it says about their relationship that they often enjoy when their partner is out of town and are less than thrilled when their partner returns home.

For some, further proof of having fallen out of love comes from how lonely they feel, how unappreciated. "Wouldn't it be nice to be with someone who doesn't take me for granted? Who finds me special? Who thinks I'm attractive?"

They have thoughts of divorce when they feel worn out from the day-to-day struggles or the tangled arguments that never get resolved. It's maddening to feel so misunderstood. It's exhausting to argue so much. They don't really want a divorce, but they think about how wonderful it might be simply not to have to negotiate *everything*. "This relationship is just too hard and too painful," they think. "Perhaps, as difficult as divorce is, it's better than staying in a tortured, loveless relationship. Maybe divorce would be better for the children. After all, isn't it worse to grow up in a household like this?"

There are also those people who worry about finding themselves attracted to someone else when they hadn't even been *thinking* about divorce. This feeling, whether actually acted upon or not, raises serious doubts in the minds of many about their love for their partner.

Equally troubling to many people is how they feel about *themselves* in the relationship. "I don't like myself," I've heard many people say. "I'm becoming a nag. I know I often speak with an edge in my voice. I don't like being that way. I feel dead. I don't show affection. I don't feel affection!"

Although all of these troubling feelings should be taken seriously, let me state from the outset that not one of them proves that love no longer exists.

Over and over again in my practice I have seen dead relationships revived. Couples tell me repeatedly that they can't believe how readily the negativity that once enveloped them could be reversed.

Of course, not all relationships can be revived. Love, as the saying goes, is blind and can lead to misperceptions and distortions of reality. Sometimes people really have made a poor choice in a partner. Other times people have developed in such diametrically opposite directions that no amount of goodwill and new behavior can bridge the gap. And then there are couples who have had so many years of negative interactions that bitterness has eroded the relationship beyond the point of repair.

Yet for most couples, the tips contained in this book will restore and strengthen their relationship surprisingly quickly.

Are Good Relationships Harder Today Than Ever Before?

Sadly, so many people I talk with informally about relationships say that they don't know anybody who has a good, long-lasting relationship. After all, when you look around, everyone seems to have problems getting along well. Many married couples stay together through thick and thin while they are miserable with each other. Is it just a matter of settling for what appears normal, or is a better relationship really possible?

Many of the couples I work with have no role models to teach them how to work through tensions and difficulties, or better yet how to preserve the love they felt for one another in the beginning. They feel as if they are sailing on uncharted waters. When they do know people (perhaps even their parents) who have a good relationship, they often feel that these relationships wouldn't work for them. Times have changed. Roles are less clearly defined. Most women with children work outside of the home in demanding jobs. Men are no longer expected to be the sole breadwinners.

Life these days is not easy. People are worried about their economic situation. Long hours and demanding, less-secure jobs add a level of stress that makes relationships even more difficult. People feel exhausted, worn out, and frayed at the edges. There's barely enough time left over after work to take a deep breath, and if you have a demanding job and children as well, forget it—there's no time for yourself, much less the relationship.

The stress of trying to do it all can easily erode a couple's relationship. It's hard to be emotionally generous and supportive when you have nothing left to give. You may know intellectually, for instance, that your husband is under a lot of pressure at work and he can't realistically say no to his boss's "request" to stay late, but yet you feel angry. You don't really want him to manage his work life differently (although sometimes you *do* think he could work shorter hours if he were more efficient) but you feel irritated nonetheless. It's just so tiring to have to handle the children all by yourself when you've been working hard all day, too. And if he does come home before the children are asleep, he keeps them up late and there's no time left for adult conversation.

People also feel deprived of time for themselves. Couples often differ in their perspective of the proper balance between individual time and time spent with their partner or the whole family. When one partner takes time away from home to see friends, engage in sports, take courses, and pursue hobbies, while the other does not, resentments can arise. Often I hear accusations of selfishness, misplaced priorities, and lack of love. On the other side, the "selfish" spouse feels that his partner is acting like a martyr, is obsessed with the children, or is controlling, manipulative, and inappropriately possessive. "It's hard to be affectionate to someone who acts like my jailer," one husband told me.

The responsibilities of parenting add to the stress. Many couples live far from their extended families and have no one to watch the children for an evening, or a night or two away. Paid baby-sitting can be expensive and has to be planned in advance, making spontaneous "dates" impossible.

Given all of these problems, it's not surprising that people find themselves attracted to others. A word about affairs: Spending time with a lover can feel like an oasis in the desert. It may be your only time to yourself and it exists in a time and space immune from the responsibilities and pressures of everyday life. It's so nice to feel love again and to have a respite from parenting and responsibilities. Affairs are confusing because even if the love and tenderness is real, there is an awareness that this isn't real life.

What *is* real, however, is the increased alienation that secret relationships produce. Ultimately, an affair is not a good solution to the stresses of family life.

Searching for True Love

Although in some ways we seem so jaded, cautious, and wary, most of us hope that lasting bonds of love and support are possible. Even those who have lived through the pain of divorce continue to want a committed, loving relationship and believe, despite their own personal experience, that good relationships are indeed possible. Young and old, previously married or not, people keep trying to find someone with whom love will last. Even those supposedly cynical veterans of failed marriages generally try again, making the leap of faith that this time marriage will work. Estimates suggest that four of every ten marriages in the United States involve a second (or more) marriage,[1] and in remarriages, more than a quarter of the people marrying are over the age of fifty.[2]

Remembering what you and your partner wished for when you decided to make a commitment helps point the way toward what you have to do to keep a relationship strong and gratifying. Here are some of the most common reasons why people fall in love and get married:

- Your loved one makes you feel special. He may make you feel smarter, funnier, prettier, and last but by no means least, more sexually attractive. He is the president of your fan club!
- Your loved one shows genuine interest in your happiness. She takes real pleasure in your triumphs.
- You feel supported emotionally. You know that you won't have to face life's difficulties alone. The future seems less frightening as part of a partnership.

- Your loved one takes a serious interest in what you think and feel.
- Your loved one is a loyal friend, your most reliable advocate.
- On a more practical level, there's the comfort of companionship. Your loved one is someone to do things with, to dream with about the house you will buy, the vacations you will take, and for many of you, the children you will raise together.

This book will give you the know-how to have the type of marriage you hoped for when you made your initial commitment to each other. We will return again and again to these basics, and I will show you, as I do with the couples I counsel, how to maintain what you have, get what you wish for, and get out of patterns that will erode love over time.

Because I have worked with so many couples and because I myself have maintained a vital marriage for such a long time while juggling a demanding career and children, people frequently ask me about the secrets to marital success. Is it mostly a matter of finding someone with whom you are truly compatible? Or are there specific things that happily married couples do to make their marriages work? The answer, I believe, is clearly the latter. Although basic compatibility is obviously important, virtually no couple is so naturally well-suited that they wouldn't have disagreements if they didn't do things to defuse conflict and build on positives. There are dozens of things harmonious couples do, not only to avoid arguments but also to keep warmth and good feelings strong. When you ask people what makes their relationship work well, they are apt to say things like "We compromise," "We respect each other," or "We give each other space." And even though this makes a lot of sense, it's hard to know exactly how to do these things yourself.

I have learned a lot from my patients and from the good times and bad in my own marriage. And it is this slowly acquired wisdom that I want to pass along to you. I will show you the nuts and bolts of relationships that continue to be gratifying over the long haul. Most books about how to improve relationships recommend elaborate exercises, pledges, contracts, and special times, places, and ways of communicating. While many of these strategies might be helpful if actually carried out, many people feel they hardly have time to handle the day-to-day chores, much less an elaborate program of restructuring their marriage. Also, these exercises can feel artificial. The tips I give you are easy to remember and easy to apply. There are no exercises or strategies. You don't have to set aside special time to improve your relationship. Instead you will learn about a way of thinking and being with one another that, like a realistic, sensible change in one's diet, is sustainable for life.

This book is about basics—how to act in a relationship so that you and your loved one remain just that to each other. And if you find yourself saying, "We love each other, but . . . ," it will help you resolve your problems so that you can say with confidence, "We love each other, *period.*"

In this book I've included many statements from couples whose concerns and feelings are probably very similar to your own. Please note that to protect the privacy of the couples I counsel, I have borrowed bits and pieces of the hundreds of stories I have heard and merged them into realistic composite portraits. The people, situations, and quotes are all accurate yet they do not refer to any specific person or couple.

I have written this book so that you can go directly to the chapters most relevant to you and the problems you are encountering in your relationship. I would suggest, however, that whatever the nature of your difficulties, you start with chapter 1:

"Four Basic Truths About What Makes Love Last." This chapter spells out the fundamental principles that will help you establish a loving atmosphere, making it easier to resolve the specific tensions described in other chapters.

Couples who think they might want to go for counseling should read "A Note for Couples Therapists," which is included in the Appendix at the end of the book. Although written for professionals, it will give you some ideas about what to look for when consulting a couples counselor.

Chapter 1

Four Basic Truths About
What Makes Love Last

It was a real question. He really wanted to know. "How did we get to this place? How did it get so bad? We started out crazy about each other, and look at us now." John was truly perplexed and sad about what his wife, Lori, had just said. She had described feeling that John wasn't very interested in her anymore. He would rather be with other people and do almost anything other than spend time alone with her. John had no real answer to this. In his heart he knew Lori was right. Deep down he thought he still loved her, but he wasn't 100 percent sure of it. He knew he *wanted* to love her. It upset him to know that he hurt her, but he didn't know how to fix what had gone wrong.

"What went wrong?" is a question I hear from almost every couple I counsel. And as often as I hear it, I am always saddened by how love can unravel if care isn't taken to preserve it.

This chapter will tell you the four basic truths about what makes relationships work well, and what can lead to the erosion of relationships that started out with solid foundations. Like all basic truths they are obvious, known by almost everyone but all too easily forgotten. Don't be deceived by their simplicity. As many of you have come to know, keeping one's eye, mind, and heart on the basics can lead to profound changes in outlook. When I describe these truths to the often very upset and angry couples I work with, the atmosphere in the room changes to one of rapt attention. There are flashes of recognition and a sense of finally understanding what had happened to their relationship.

This chapter lays out the building blocks for a successful relationship. Just as I do with the couples who see me in my office, I will tell you how to translate these basic truths into new ways of interacting so that you and your spouse feel truly loved and appreciated.

Truth #1: We Love Those Who Make Us Feel Good About Ourselves

If you remember this one point, you will get enough out of this book to give your marriage a good shot at success. And in my experience working with couples whose marriages are in trouble, this simple truth is frequently ignored.

Richard and Jackie came to me for counseling after feeling disillusioned with their seven-year marriage. Jackie, a thirty-four-year-old accountant, works long hours "for not enough money." Before work she struggles to get three-year-old Amanda up, dressed, and fed quickly so that she can drop her at nursery school before going to work. Richard, a thirty-five-year-old electrical engineer, works in a distant suburb. He leaves the house before Jackie and Amanda are out of bed. When he gets home at about seven P.M., the baby-sitter leaves and he starts dinner so that they can eat when Jackie gets home at eight or eight-thirty.

In a recent session, Jackie shrugged and said half-apologetically, "It's hard to explain what's bothering me. I know my husband loves me, but at my office and with friends—in fact, just about anywhere else—I feel like I get a more positive response than I do from him. Sometimes I think I'm being childish when I want him to compliment me—Richard certainly thinks I am. I know when you've been together as long as we have it's not realistic to want your husband to go gaga over you, but still I'm worried because I feel better when I'm away from him than when I'm with him. I think the problem may be me. It's not as if I think he doesn't love me. Maybe I just need too much ego-stroking."

"I feel the same way," said Richard. "But I tell myself to grow up. This is real life, not a romance novel. Everyone in my office thinks I'm great, not only because of the work I do but because they think I'm a decent guy. I'm the one everyone tells their problems to. But at home all I hear is how inattentive I am when Jackie's talking, how I don't do my share of the housework, or how I'm not 'nurturant'—whatever that is!"

These are not the only reasons Jackie and Richard have come to see me. This feeling of being unappreciated is just one of the concerns that emerge when I ask them to tell me what has lead them to seek couples counseling. Like so many couples who come to see me, Richard and Jackie are committed to each other and want nothing more than to provide their child with a happy and secure home. They both say with conviction that they love each other. They get along well most of the time, but when a fight erupts it gets out of hand. "Once we get going in an argument," Richard said, "it's scary how much rage seems bottled up, just waiting for a chance to come out."

My response is that they should feel concerned, both about the rage and the underlying feeling of not being sufficiently appreciated. Over time, that feeling can erode the love they still have for each other.

In my first session with a couple I always ask them to think back to how they made each other feel in the beginning of their relationship. Most couples remember feeling admired, appreciated, valued. Think back to the beginning of your own relationship. Perhaps your spouse thought your sense of humor was wonderfully outrageous. Or that you seemed to be able to talk to just about anybody. Or that you were a walking encyclopedia. Perhaps you thought that he was fantastically creative. Or smart. Or nurturant.

You and your partner may have fallen in love slowly and cautiously. Not many people have the head-over-heels movie experience. In fact, you each may have been quite aware of the other's shortcomings and deficiencies. Yet in spite of this, most of the time you made each other feel that some pretty special traits were recognized and valued.

So many people I speak with both professionally and informally wish they could recapture that falling-in-love feeling they had in the beginning of their relationship. There is really nothing quite like it—the high of sensing that someone is crazy about you and appreciates your uniqueness, the exhilaration that comes with knowing that you both feel the same way, the pleasurably charged quality to every interaction.

We all know that we can't expect to have that courtship feeling in our day-to-day lives. Sure, a romantic holiday can reignite the flames somewhat, but it's never quite the same as in the beginning of the relationship. Some couples do occasionally revisit those moments of romantic intensity through fierce fighting and equally passionate reconciliations. But no matter how sweet the reconciliations, riding a roller coaster of this sort dangerously undermines relationships.

Clearly I cannot tell you how to bring back that exquisite feeling of romance you had in the beginning of your relationship. I do believe, however, that you can maintain the fundamental feeling of mutual admiration. In strong relationships, couples continue to give each other ego boosts from time to time, which provide a low voltage charge reminiscent of the early days of the relationship.

Many people tell me that they have become upset about their marriage when they catch a glimpse of couples who seem close, tender, and interested in each other. Simply observing an ordinary interaction sets off feelings of sadness and the awareness that something precious has been lost along the way. Sarah, a woman in her midthirties, described sitting across the aisle from a married couple in their sixties who talked together during an entire hour-and-a-half train ride. The interest they seemed to have in one another left Sarah feeling disturbed about her own marriage. Sarah and her husband didn't argue much, but they sure didn't seem nearly as interested in each other as did this couple, who probably had been together many more years. David, who stated that he loved his wife of twenty-five years, was envious of a young colleague whose wife always had breakfast with him so they would have some quiet time to talk before the kids got up. Observing couples in new relationships often evokes wistful longing, despite the fact that you know the couple is in that special stage of love. One woman came to see me after watching the wonderful interaction between her daughter and her daughter's fiancé. It became clear to the woman just how matter-of-fact her own relationship had become. Though pleased for her daughter, she felt sad for herself.

Are couples who continue to admire each other over stretches of time just lucky to have found one another? My work with couples has taught me that this is not simply a matter of good fortune. Though a lucky few have genuinely found their soul mates, most couples *could* give each other that feeling of appreciation if *they simply thought to do so*.

Perhaps this will sound strange, but I have come to the conclusion that many couples just don't know they need to make sure their partner continues to feel admired. Some never thought about it. Others hold the mistaken notion that when you are married you ought to be able to assume that you hold each other in high regard, and that verbalizing it seems superfluous.

Expressing Admiration Goes Beyond Saying I Love You

Scene: A couple in bed at night after spending the evening helping the kids with homework, paying bills, preparing lunches for the next day, and watching a little television.

WIFE: Do you love me?

HUSBAND: (with a bit of annoyance in his voice) Of course.

WIFE: Why do you say it with that tone?

HUSBAND: Because I've told you over and over again and you keep asking.

WIFE: I know you tell me, but it sounds so matter-of-fact, and usually it's after I've said it first.

HUSBAND: But you *know* I love you. Why would I be here if I didn't love you?

WIFE: Yeah, I guess I know you love me, but *why* do you love me?

HUSBAND: I just do, that's all. Now can we stop talking about it? I really need to get to sleep.

WIFE: I mean it. I want to know. *Why* do you love me?

HUSBAND: You're caring. You're nice. I just love you. Now come on, you know I love you.

Lights out.

The wife in my little scenario is not really uncertain of her husband's love. She's not craving an "I love you," but more specific feedback. After a stressful day in the office and a full evening of mommying, she needs a little ego-stroking. She wants someone to pay attention to her, to make her feel good about herself, to give her a pat on the back. She's feeling unnoticed, unknown except in her role as mother and wife. Even when her husband reaches out to her she experiences his desire for sexual contact as not about her, but simply about his physical needs. She just happens to be the body in bed next to him.

Ironically her husband probably feels the same way. People at work think of him as clever, funny, warm, and a lovable nut when it comes to his passion for hockey. Like his wife, he feels unknown at home, unnoticed. And like his wife he knows he is loved but that love doesn't translate into anything that strokes his ego. He tries to connect to his wife through sexual contact but often she seems tired, indifferent, and distracted. She doesn't seem overwhelmed by his skill as a lover—to say the least! The husband who feels this way might not ask "Do you love me?" It is not really the right question, anyway. Instead he might complain that his wife doesn't seem interested at all in his work. Or he might withdraw. Or he might be irritable. He might not be able to put his finger on what is bothering him. All he knows is that somehow he doesn't feel so great when he's at home.

How to make your partner feel good about himself/herself even when a lot of what he/she does is annoying and disappointing. Many of the couples who come to see me have felt negatively toward their spouse for quite some time. They feel disappointed, frustrated, and certainly in no frame of mind to admire their partner. Often they feel more like the foreman of a jury that is recommending a guilty verdict than they do the president of their partner's fan club. By the time couples find themselves in a therapist's office, their ability or willingness to make each other feel good about themselves has greatly diminished. Yet with a little direction, even these couples can soon begin giving each other some of the admiration that they so desperately desire.

How is that possible? I'm going to tell you what you can easily do at home, but first I'd like to show you a scene from my office.

When counseling couples, I begin the first session by asking each person to tell me what concerns him about their marriage. I ask for details so that I can get a sense of the type of interactions that upset them. Then I tell the couple that I'd like to put these concerns on the back burner for a while so that I can see these problems in the larger context of their relationship. I want to know what, if anything, still goes right despite these difficulties. I want to know if there are times when they can still have some fun together. And perhaps most important of all, I want to know what made them fall in love with each other in the first place—and if they can still see any signs of these qualities.

This conversation takes place in response to my asking Vicki what made her fall in love with her husband.

VICKI: I was temping for the advertising agency where he was an account manager. I noticed him in the cafeteria with a group of people and frankly, I liked his looks. He was cute, kind of boyish-looking. I'm not the type to go over to someone and probably nothing would have happened if he hadn't started talking to me on the elevator one day. One thing led to another and we moved in with each other about six months after we met.

THERAPIST: So you were initially attracted to him because he was cute. As you got to know him better, what was it about him that drew you to him, that led you to grow closer and closer?

VICKI: Hmm . . . I haven't thought about that for a long time. Let me think. Well, I know I liked how many friends he had and that he seemed to go out of his way for them. He really cared about them, and he was eager for me to meet them. He had an easy manner with people, and I liked that. I'm not that way at all.

THERAPIST: Was there anything else about him that drew you to him besides his friendly and caring way with people?

VICKI: Well, we liked the same things and had fun together doing a lot of crazy stuff. And we seemed to have the same values. I felt like I could just have fun hanging out with him. We didn't need to be doing anything special to have fun with each other.

THERAPIST: Anything else? What made him seem like a good person to marry?

VICKI: I felt that he really liked kids and wanted to have a family as much as I did.

THERAPIST: Here's what I want you to think about. I know that the two of you have had quite a bad time with each other for several years now. Despite all the trouble you've been having, do you ever see any of the things you just described? Do they still exist at all? Like his caring way with people, or the ability to have fun just spending time together. Or the same values.

VICKI: Sure I do. He's still awfully good with people. Everybody loves him. He has a million friends.

THERAPIST: Is anything else still there?

VICKI: I think we have basically the same values and once

in a while, if we manage to avoid a power struggle, we can have some fun together.

THERAPIST: Can you say a little more about your husband's way with people? It sounds as if you think he's especially good at it. What does he actually do that you admire?

VICKI: He has a way of warmly and affectionately teasing friends that makes each person feel special. I'm not good at that and he's a master at it.

As Vicki and I talk about what she still admires and sees positively despite all the tension, her husband's posture relaxes. He turns toward her with a slight smile on his face. Clearly it's been years since he's heard any of this.

The session proceeds as I ask the husband the same questions. And as he admiringly describes Vicki's great capacity to enjoy life and the enthusiastic and energetic way that she approached change, Vicki's face softens as she shyly grins.

Obviously this brief exchange has not solved the couple's problems. But they have walked out of my office feeling a bit closer and more optimistic than they had an hour before.

How does this apply to you? Understanding that you don't have to totally approve of or admire your partner to be able to share your feelings about what you *do* admire can help you avoid getting to the point where you have to seek couples counseling. Even couples who have negative feelings about one another can usually recognize that they still truly admire some of their partner's qualities.

For example, let's say that as you and your wife approach your parked car you see a police officer standing there, pad in hand, about to write out a ticket for an expired meter. Your wife races up and uses all of her social know-how to convince the police officer to put his ticket pad away.

Even if you and your wife have been angry at one another, you can still admire her for this ability. A comment about how she can charm the pants off anybody can help create an atmosphere that encourages the resolution of conflicts, anger, and hurt feelings. I find that it is sometimes helpful for couples to think about how they interact with their children as compared to how they interact with each other. Most people recognize that even though children may do many annoying things, parents still need to praise and recognize their children's positive attributes. Too often couples withhold positive feedback because they think it has been canceled out by disappointments. But withholding admiration and praise because you are angry at your partner is just plain destructive. The more that each of you withholds praise, the more alienated from each other you will become.

How to convey admiration year after year without getting repetitive. What happens after you've told your partner what you admire about him? You can't keep saying the same things over and over again, because it would become meaningless and lose the power to give that little ego boost that brings you and your partner closer. Here's the trick to giving positive feedback year after year after year.

First, *practice noticing interactions and behaviors that you like and admire.* Most of us do not do this naturally. We tend to focus on what's going wrong rather than on what's going right. But this does not mean that we cannot learn to do so. No more than a handful of many hundreds of clients have not been able to greatly increase their ability to notice positives when they make a conscious effort in that direction. With practice you can easily develop a keen eye for such behaviors. This is much easier to do than you realize. When you stop reading this, if you consciously try to observe positives in your partner you will see a lot more than you thought was there.

Second, *use specific observations to give credibility and power to general statements of admiration.* Perhaps you noticed that in my therapy room scenario, Vicki broke down her general admiration into a specific observation. She stated that her husband is good at affectionate teasing. Your spouse will find your feedback fresh and meaningful if you provide details. For example, perhaps you feel your husband has a good sense of humor. A statement such as "It was great the way you got Jimmy to try something new by joking with him—you really have a terrific sense of humor" will mean a lot more to him than simply saying "I think you have a good sense of humor." Or perhaps you notice how your wife spoke to one of her close friends about something that annoyed her, rather than brushing it under the rug the way you tend to do. A statement like "I'm impressed with the way you handled that situation with Sandra. You really know how to be forceful without alienating people" means a lot more than "You're good with people."

Let's return to our bedtime scenario. If the husband had mentioned something earlier in the evening about his wife's knack for handling their difficult child—specifically, how well she handled a situation that evening that could have lead to a tantrum—I guarantee that the wife would not have been asking "Do you love me?"

So if your spouse is generally good at getting conversations going, telling jokes, keeping confidences, or sticking to an exercise regime, notice instances of these traits and let her know that you've noticed. Or if you are impressed with your partner's ability to stay calm in a crisis, or his creative solutions for tackling difficult problems, or her confidence in cooking without a recipe, or his knack of finding good buys, or his taste in clothes, or her ability to remember what she read in the newspaper, let him or her know that you admire these abilities.

You may wonder why you should admire your partner when he doesn't admire you. The short answer is that the saying "What goes around comes around" is usually true. When one person in a relationship starts to be more positive, the vicious cycle of hurt and withholding begins to break. *But if this is a sticking point, and you just can't see yourself giving this kind of feedback, then I suggest you skip to chapter 6, which deals with what to do when things have gotten very bad between you and your spouse.*

Truth #2: Most of Us Know What Will Warm Our Partner's Heart

The first counseling session with Kathy and Bob was nearing the end. Kathy had spoken with anger and bitterness about Bob's selfishness. She felt that he had never adjusted to being part of a family, and made decisions on the basis of what was best for him individually. She had become deeply disappointed in the marriage. It hurt her that Bob's career always came first. And though she knew he did love their two kids, he participated very little in family life. "I assume he loves me, too," she had said earlier, "but I don't *feel* it."

Bob was fed up. "I break my butt trying to make a good living and all I get is complaints. The moment I come home she starts in with the list of things I should do or didn't do. She gets on a roll about how irresponsible I am for coming home late. She just doesn't get it . . . *I work these hours because I need to.* All I ever get is criticism."

About halfway through the session I asked the couple if they could put these complaints on hold for the rest of the meeting so that I could get a sense of what had attracted them to each other and what was still good in the relationship despite all of the hurt, anger, and disappointment. It had been years since Kathy and Bob had actually talked about what they loved, liked, and admired about each other. They exchanged shy, cautious glances and half-smiles as they talked. The atmosphere warmed noticeably. My job as the therapist was to keep it going, to build on the tiny bit of goodwill and warmth that had been achieved in the last fifteen or twenty minutes.

Here's what I said to them and what I am saying to you: *We all know what warms our partner's heart if we stop to think about it.* Doing more of what draws your partner to you strengthens the relationship. For one person it might be expressing appreciation for hard work. For another it might be taking pleasure in his spouse's sense of humor. The point is that we all do know what touches the heart of our partner.

When people are angry and hurt they gradually stop doing the things that make their partner feel warmly toward them. Often this happens without any plan or conscious decision. Few of us actually decide to withhold or punish, though of course this can happen. Rather, when we feel hurt and angry it just doesn't occur to us to be emotionally generous.

I asked Kathy and Bob if they knew what they could do to create warmth between them. Kathy said that she had thought of something. I asked her not to say it aloud but rather to try it out at home. It's really much better to just do it, not talk about it. Talking about it can take away some of the pleasure that the other person experiences, because the actions can seem contrived.

Bob was not so sure what would make Kathy soften toward him. I asked him to search his memory for times, perhaps going years back, when Kathy seemed really touched by something he did. He smiled as he remembered how she used to love the strange little notes he would leave in odd places. And once he practically bought out the apology section of the card shop when he had done something inexcusable.

"Those things wouldn't do it anymore" said Kathy. "There's too much water under the bridge and I need to see some actions, not notes and cards."

"See what I mean?" said Bob. "Nothing I can do will make her warm toward me."

"That's not true. I loved it when I knew you were really thinking about me when I wasn't there. You used to bring home little treats for me once in a while or call me during the day just to chat. Thing like that really mean something to me."

There are two important points to remember about warming each other's heart:

1. The gestures should be small, doable, and not extravagant.
2. Make the gesture a part of your everyday interactions.

Sure, sending dozens of roses will generally get a big response; so will planning a surprise party, or a romantic weekend away, or giving some expensive gift. But it isn't necessary to make such big gestures, and often, thinking that this is the kind of thing you have to do gets in the way of doing the small, day-to-day things that ultimately mean even more.

And remember: *You do not have to be feeling great about each other to do the things that warm each other's heart.* What you do need is goodwill and a desire to have a loving relationship.

So, think about it right now. Do you get a special smile from your wife when you remind her to take her vitamins? If you tell your partner that he should give himself a break and sleep a little later tomorrow, does it seem to warm his heart? If your partner is stressed out about work and you suggest that she spend some time in the evening or on the weekend catching up, does she seem very appreciative? If you cook your partner's favorite dish, which you haven't made in a long time, or come home from the supermarket with the type of cookies she loved when she was a child, or offer to do one of your partner's chores because he is having a hard few weeks, you will be strengthening the love you have for one another.

Do you see what I mean? You probably know a lot of things you could do to make your partner feel closer to you.

Whether or not your relationship feels a little rocky, it is important to remember that love needs daily nourishment.

• • •

Let's get back to Kathy and Bob. In the next session they reported that they had had a pretty bad argument when Bob told Kathy at the last minute that he was planning to go into the office Saturday afternoon. They both noted that this fight differed from others in that it didn't ruin the whole weekend. On Sunday they went biking with the kids, and everyone got along pretty well. Even the kids fought less than they normally did.

When I asked how they had implemented the idea of warming each other's hearts, Bob said that he noticed that, apart from the fight, Kathy was being nicer to him. She offered to make him breakfast one morning when he had to leave the house an hour earlier than usual. "I was shocked—I would never dream of asking her to do that, with her busy schedule. But it felt really nice. She got it! It's a real pain having to leave so early, and I felt as if she were trying to make it a little easier."

"I'm glad he noticed but I can't say he did much to warm *my* heart," Kathy laughingly said. "But he wasn't being particularly bad, either—except for that business of working on Saturday."

"Yeah, I guess I forgot about it. You're right."

It's important to be realistic. When one person breaks the cycle of withholding, it is not a magic solution. Fights will still occur and your partner is unlikely to respond in kind immediately. Nonetheless I hope you can see from this real-life example that the atmosphere of tension in a relationship begins to soften even when only one person acts emotionally generous. Somehow Kathy and Bob were able to let go of their argument a bit sooner. And in the next session Bob recognized that he had not done his share to create an atmosphere of warmth and love. Eventually there must be reciprocity, but you must be patient.

Truth #3: Criticism Erodes Love

When Melissa and Steven first started dating they were delighted at how well they seemed to understand each other. Within a few weeks each felt as if they had found their soul mate. They could talk about anything, from movies to their most intense anxieties. Strong trust developed between them and they could say anything to one another—even critical things. They knew the criticism was in the context of love, and though it sometimes hurt they didn't view it as a problem in the relationship. Melissa talked to Steven about how he tended to interrupt people in conversations. She understood that he had grown up in a family in which no one ever let anyone else finish a sentence. She was concerned that this habit could get in the way of his career if he wasn't careful. There were other things that she thought he should change—when he started to eat before everyone had been served, or spoke with his mouth full.

Melissa also gave Steven feedback of a deeper sort. She pointed out how argumentative he could be with certain people and that he seemed to have trouble handling authority. Almost everything that Melissa said was well received. Steven had never spoken so much about himself—Melissa was really able to bring him out. She took such an interest in him and most of what she had to say seemed to be on target.

> TIME: Eight years later
> SCENE: My office
> STEVEN: *Everything* I do is wrong. I have no common sense! I don't think! I don't care about anyone but myself! That's all I hear. All she does is criticize me. She says she wants a more equal relationship when it comes to child care, but when she comes home from work she gives me the third degree about how much time I actually spent with each kid and how much time I let them watch videos. Then she starts in on me about what I fed the kids and quizzes me about the chores I didn't get to. I get a pit in my stomach when she walks through the door.
> MELISSA: I don't know if he's just stubborn, but no matter how many times I tell him something he doesn't seem to learn! I really feel he's being passive-aggressive—he's purposely not doing it the way he should, out of spite. It's not just how he is with the kids. It's a lot of things. I think he purposely stacks the dishwasher the wrong way. And I'm embarrassed by the way he talks to the baby-sitter. He's just not polite.

What happened to Melissa and Steve happens all too often to many couples. Melissa may well be right that Steven's failure to learn is passive-aggressive. He clearly is annoyed by how critical Melissa can be. A vicious cycle has developed in which Melissa keeps criticizing and Steven continues "forgetting."

How did two people who started out with all the goodwill and love in the world find themselves living out roles that both of them dislike? As with every couple, their story is complicated. Trying to juggle the pressures that go with a two-career family and children led them to neglect the basics of a loving relationship. Like many couples they no longer gave each other much admiration and seldom did what I call warming each other's heart. One of the only things that remained from the early days of their relationship was Melissa's criticism. In the context of intense love and romance, people can be pretty good-natured about constructive criticism. But hundreds of couples have told me that the most troubling part of their relationship is feeling the constant and often deep criticism.

It is important to understand that Melissa and Steven fell into this problematic pattern *together*, and that neither of them is solely to blame for what has happened. Melissa thought it was helpful to criticize, and Steven, instead of telling her that it bothered him, protested by ignoring Melissa's requests, demands, and advice.

I am an amateur painter and when I do portraits from photographs, my husband knows that I welcome his input. I listen when he tells me that the angle of the head doesn't look quite the same as the angle in the photo, or that the skin color seems off to him. Often he is right and I find that another set of eyes is helpful. But sometimes when I've been working hard at a painting I feel I've had enough of his input! I've done the best I can and the painting is as good as it's going to be. Saying "Enough!" to him tactfully but firmly has helped him know when any further comments will be more irritating than helpful.

In my experience the willingness to accept criticism seems to erode over time. Perhaps the biggest complaint I hear from couples is that they feel constantly scrutinized and evaluated.

What was acceptable during the courtship stage of the relationship rapidly begins to feel undermining and negative. When you become your partner's critic instead of the president of his fan club, you are headed for trouble.

Some of you may be thinking, "Yes, she's right! I've got to let some things go. I should be more easygoing. I've become a nag. I have to mellow out and not be so perfectionistic." But I am not suggesting that you accept everything about your partner. Being less critical does not mean you should let yourself be mistreated or taken advantage of. It does mean two things, however. First, criticism is *not* the way to get your partner to change. And second, you need to be very selective about what you do criticize. Before you say something ask yourself, "Is this really important?" For most couples, even one criticism a day is too much. The fewer criticisms the better. It will help you to stop criticizing if you remember that changing your partner through criticism simply has not worked and the more you do it the less effective it is. If you try to minimize criticism and at the same time communicate what you *do* admire, you have a much better chance of being heard. And if you add to this equation being really conscious of doing the things that warm your partner's heart, you will create an atmosphere of love and goodwill in which difficult problems can be solved.

Perhaps this sounds all well and good but you wonder how you can possibly stop criticizing when your spouse does so many things that really annoy you. Perhaps you are thinking, "I criticize for good reason and it seems unrealistic to just stop." If you are eager to find out how to really get him or her to listen, please skip ahead to chapter 3. But do remember that the advice given in later chapters will work much better if you have laid the groundwork by starting to warm each other's heart. It only takes one of you to break a pattern of emotional withholding and I hope this chapter will have convinced you to take the first step.

Truth #4: There Is No Such Thing As Unshakable, Immutable, Affair-Resistant Love

Some of you may object strongly to what I'm going to say next. You will say I'm too cynical or lack faith in the strength of marital vows. But I believe that no marriage or relationship is safe from the threat of an affair. No one can rest assured that their partner will stay faithful to them. Over and over again I have seen the most upstanding citizens, with strong religious convictions and moral codes, override their own value system because they cannot resist the power of love and infatuation. Sometimes people do manage to refrain from acting on their feelings but the affair of the heart is every bit as powerful and threatening to committed relationships as one that becomes sexual. No matter how devoted and caring your partner may be today, he or she can change.

A Cautionary Tale

Valerie met Gregory when she was a sophomore in high school and he was a senior. Having emigrated to the United States from Budapest only one year earlier, she had few American friends and was grateful for all the support and encouragement he gave her. What started out as a friendship soon turned into a passionate teenage love affair. Valerie's parents were outraged by what they regarded as promiscuous behavior. They sent her away to relatives for the summer, and that autumn Gregory went off to college. Gregory was an unusually mature and solid young man. He was calm and persistent and "talked sense" into Valerie when she was so angry at her parents that she seriously contemplated running away. Whenever he was home from college he would visit Valerie, and the respectful way he treated her parents eventually led them to see him as a fine young man.

Over the years Valerie and Gregory sometimes thought that they should each go out with other people simply because they had been each other's first and only love. But after a few weeks apart they always concluded that they were extraordinarily lucky to have found one another and that it was silly to put themselves through a separation just because they had met so young.

Gregory had always wanted to be a physician and went to medical school right after graduating from college. The four years of medical school were difficult ones. Valerie's father became terminally ill during that time and died a few months before Gregory graduated. During his illness Valerie became quite despondent. Gregory did his best to juggle the demands of medical school with his deep concern for how Valerie was feeling. It upset him that Valerie was often angry and irritable with him and accused him of not being there for her. Valerie was an intense person, and though Gregory sometimes found her extreme anger or sadness frightening he always was able to help her overcome whatever bothered her. But ever since her father became ill she seemed mad at him almost all the time. Gregory understood that she was going through a very hard time and believed that eventually she would become her old self again.

They married shortly after Gregory completed medical school. An excellent student, he graduated with honors despite the fact that he frequently went home for the weekend to be with Valerie. Gregory wanted to do his internship and residency out west, and when they first got engaged they both looked forward to the adventure of being newlyweds in parts unknown. But understanding that Valerie needed to be near her bereaved mother, he agreed without resentment to do his internship and residency at a New York hospital instead.

Valerie had complete faith in Gregory's love for her. Though she was often irritated with him for becoming preoccupied with his studies and ambitions and felt sometimes that he didn't pay enough attention to her, she believed that his love for her was absolute and unshakable. He was her best friend, he was completely trustworthy, and he was a deeply moral and spiritual person. Had he not fallen in love with Valerie he might even have considered the priesthood.

I'll never forget my first meeting with Valerie and Gregory. Married fourteen years, they had two children and plenty of money. An internationally known pediatric surgeon, Gregory devoted much of his professional life to working with the Red Cross and the United Nations to provide the best medical care possible to poor children all over the world. A few months before coming to see me, while getting his clothes ready for summer storage at the cleaners Valerie had come across love letters addressed to Gregory. Valerie had so much trust in Gregory that when he told her they were from the mentally disturbed mother of one of his child patients she believed him. Three weeks later when she heard him whispering into the phone late at night she became suspicious. After days of questioning and many denials Gregory finally admitted that he had been having an affair for over two years.

In the next few weeks Valerie lost nearly twenty pounds. She was clinically depressed. She couldn't eat, sleep, or concentrate on her work. And though Gregory swore that he had broken off his relationship with his lover, Valerie was profoundly distrustful and felt that she could never recover from this betrayal. Like many people, Valerie had believed that her partner's love for her was immutable. She had always had 100 percent trust in him and regarded him as the most morally principled person she had ever encountered. She believed that he would never want to hurt her. She couldn't comprehend that he had deceived her all this time and had manipulated and purposely misled her when she asked if something was wrong. Valerie described feeling, prior to this discovery, that Gregory's love for her was as solid as a parent's love. Of course she knew that they had been having problems, and clearly they should have sought couples counseling long ago. Yet she believed that the fights, disappointments, and misunderstandings could not affect their basic love. It was unthinkable.

This was neither the first nor the last time I have heard people say pretty much the same thing.

So how did it happen? The long and short of it is that Gregory and Valerie stopped giving each other the admiration, recognition, and emotional support that nourishes love. Gregory was admired tremendously by almost everyone who came in contact with him. He was a warm, highly competent doctor who really cared about the children on whom he operated. Valerie loved and admired him as well but for years she had felt neglected and taken for granted. Though she tried to support his ambitious career, she felt that the years he spent in training had taken a tremendous toll on the relationship. She didn't work outside the home when the children were young, and with Gregory's long hours she often felt like a single parent. When she went back to work full-time she felt as if she, too, received more admiration from her coworkers. She resented that Gregory seemed more devoted to his patients than to their family. It was hard to criticize him because his work was so important, yet she felt neglected and unappreciated. When Gregory was at home she had trouble warming up to him. She knew that she had a pretty sharp tongue and often spoke to him sarcastically. Valerie became emotionally withholding. She stopped confiding in him and rarely expressed affection. When he tried to be sexually intimate with her she found that she just wasn't in the mood. Valerie and Gregory became more and more alienated. They no longer made each other feel good about themselves.

How do I explain how a man as basically good as Gregory could have an affair? I'll talk more about affairs in chapter 6, but in essence I believe that the wish to be loved and to feel you add joy to another person's life is one of the most powerful human motivators. People will lie, rationalize, and distort the truth—to themselves and to their partner—to have this need fulfilled. The moral of this story is that *you must never forget that* any *relationship can fall apart*. But this knowledge does not have to lead to distrust and anxiety. Instead it can help you make sure that you act upon the basic truths laid out in this chapter.

I often hear people say that the worst part of their marital difficulties is the feeling that they are the primary source of unhappiness in their partner's life. It is terribly disheartening to believe that you cause more upset than pleasure. Letting your partner know the ways in which he is a positive force in your life helps strengthen the bond. In combination with the other suggestions in this chapter, it is the best way to inoculate your relationship against the danger of new loves.

Chapter 2

We Love Each Other, But . . . Every Decision Is a Tug-of-war

Many couples experience life with their partner as a tug-of-war. The following situations illustrate some common frustrations:

- "We moved into our apartment over a year ago and we still have almost no furniture and have to eat off snack tables. It's not that we can't afford furniture; it's just that I like the antique pine look and he likes real modern stuff, so we end up getting nothing."
- "I want to live in the suburbs and she loves the city, so we don't make any decision either way. We live in a really cramped space but I can't get her to agree to move."
- "Planning a vacation is just about impossible. We get into big fights. I really want to sit on the beach all day and she wants to travel around, which I hate."
- "Sundays are awful. The day just disappears. The kids get cranky. We never get going until late in the afternoon. It takes us hours to decide what we are doing."
- "It's hard to find something to do when we go out. I hate the thrillers that he always wants to see and he hates the romantic movies that I tend to like."

- "I'm a morning person and he's a night person. I find it very frustrating that on the weekends he stays up until three A.M. and then doesn't get up until noon. Half the day is shot by the time we get out of the house to do something."
- "We just never seem to want the same thing at the same time."

Does this sound familiar? Do you and your partner feel that though you love each other your differences make it hard to live together? This chapter will tell you how to manage these differences without either of you feeling defeated, bullied, or disappointed.

Being Afraid to Join

Many of the people who consult with me are terribly concerned about losing their independence. They are committed to one another but equally committed to their own autonomy. I believe that preserving a sense of separateness and individuality helps to keep relationships vital and interesting.

Yet finding the right balance between the "I" and the "we" is a tricky business. If every decision is put through the test of evaluating how "I," as an independent and separate individual, feel about something, the couple is likely to find themselves disagreeing quite often. Seldom will two "I"s want exactly the same thing. Many people resist the impulse to say "Fine," or "It's up to you," or "It really doesn't matter much to me, so you decide," because they fear that an easygoing attitude will threaten their sense of self. Some couples use their different opinions as a way of handling their fear of becoming excessively close, dependent, and merged with one another. But instead of keeping some sense of separateness by developing their own interests, careers, and friendships, they use decision-making as an opportunity to assert their individuality.

Recently one of my clients complained of his wife's constant need to assert her independence. He knew he risked sounding politically incorrect as he said: "She can never just go along with what I want. I know I'm not supposed to think this way, but sometimes I wish she'd just be a 'wife' and do something because it's important to me. Of course I admire her strength and independence; they are the qualities that attracted me to her in the first place. But is it *all* about independence? I grew up thinking that a husband and wife were a team, a unit. We're never a unit. My wife and I act almost like business partners who have to negotiate everything. I know this is what marriages are like these days but sometimes our interaction feels so cold and unfriendly. Maybe it's because I'm fourteen years older than she is and more old-fashioned than I thought."

I don't believe that this couple's problems are about feminism. Just as often, the man is reluctant to "join." Many men feel controlled if they go along with their wife's suggestions. Women often say to me, "He always has to take the opposite side," or "He won't do it if *I* suggest it."

Being Agreeable

Here are two ways to think about issues so that you can avoid unnecessary conflict. First, ask yourself honestly: "Do I really care?" If you really don't care very much one way or the other then don't use this decision as an opportunity to define your-self.

For instance, suppose your husband says that he wants to hang a poster on the bathroom door. He clearly likes the poster but knows that since you share the space he needs to check it out with you first. Rather than automatically asking yourself if you like this poster, first ask yourself whether it really matters to you at all. Perhaps you will decide that it doesn't matter much, because it's not in an area of the house that anybody sees but the two of you. Unless you will really hate looking at it every day, it may not be worth making an independent decision about this issue.

Or let's say your wife asks what you think about having some of her friends from work over for a barbecue. Though you think these people are perfectly nice, they aren't really your friends. Instead of asking if you really want to entertain these people, you might decide that it's no big deal to have a barbecue and even though this is not what *you* would have chosen to do, it will probably be a pleasant-enough day.

You do not need to evaluate *every* decision on the basis of how you feel about it as an individual. People use all sorts of little things as an opportunity to assert their individuality and to declare how different they are from their spouse.

Also, remind yourself that another valid aspect of your decision can be the pleasure it gives you to know that your partner will be happy with the choice. Preserving your individuality while still part of a couple does not mean that it is wrong to include the wish to please your partner as an important element in your choice.

Of course, not all conflicts can be avoided this easily. Certain issues really matter to both of you and you will need to reach some sort of agreement.

Seduction Versus the Sledgehammer

"We had a big argument last night," said Kim. "Everytime Carl and I try to talk about where we are going to live when the new baby comes, we get nowhere. He just gets mad and walks away.

Our apartment is overflowing right now with Alec's toys and other stuff. Where are we supposed to put the baby? We just can't stay where we are."

"I'm a city person," explains Carl. "When she says we have to do something about where we are going to live, I know she means moving to a big house in the country—*she* calls it the suburbs—and I hate that idea. It depresses me. But she pushes and pushes and refuses to acknowledge how much I would hate it. There's no point in talking to her—she's made up her mind and I'm just supposed to get with the program."

Does this sound familiar? I have heard this type of stalemate hundreds and hundreds of times. Carl and Kim have each taken a position they feel strongly about, and there doesn't seem to be any give. When they attempt to talk about the issue they get stuck. Kim asserts that "Kids need space and land to run around on," and Carl says "I can't do it. It would kill me. People bring up kids in the city, too."

The Importance of Elaboration

Again, what I am going to say may seem obvious. Yet in my work with couples I have been astounded by how often people are stuck in opposing positions, in part because they do not elaborate enough on the various components of their preference. When you provide more details about how you think about the issue, you may say something that strikes a receptive note in your partner. You may plant a seed that could grow and make the choice you hope for more appealing to your partner.

In a counseling session, I asked Kim to tell Carl why having a big house outside of the city appealed to her. "I picture each of us having our own space in the house and more time to do what we want because the kids will be able to go out and play by themselves and we won't have to take them on play dates. I also love the idea that we would have room for overnight guests. And I thought we might eventually be able to build a pool—I picture us hanging out on the deck together while the kids play in the backyard."

"If we stay in the city," said Carl, "we could take the kids on all kinds of cultural excursions on the weekends. I love the idea of exposing them to different foods and people. And I'd be able to take time off from work easily to go to things at school, because I'd be nearby. Also, walking to work every day is great exercise and we won't have to depend on a car all the time."

Couples often wrongly assume that their partner already knows the appealing components of their choice. Clearly, your partner knows *some* of the reasons you feel the way you do, but I have found it helps a great deal when the reasons behind your preferences are spelled out in more detail. Sometimes some small thing will catch the attention of your partner.

For instance, Carl did like Kim's idea that they would each have some space in the house for themselves, and that they would have more time for separate activities because they wouldn't need to supervise the children as much. He knew, of course, that houses require a lot of upkeep, and that he would also probably spend a lot of time coaching the kids' teams. But still, it *would* be nice to have his own study and good for the kids to be able to go out and play by themselves. And Kim found it appealing that Carl would be more available to go to school events if they lived in the city.

By sparking the imagination of your partner rather than stubbornly trying to push your ideas, differences have a better chance of getting resolved. Please do not misunderstand me: the brief conversation described above did not completely resolve the conflict between Kim and Carl. But it did begin the process of communication and compromise.

Even Lawyers Aren't Always Adversarial

All too often, couples who cannot resolve their differences approach each other like bad lawyers. They think that if they argue their point long and hard enough they will wear the other person down. Even when that strategy works it is not healthy for relationships to have a winner and a loser. Ultimately both parties lose when one person feels defeated.

Many lawyers I have worked with tell me that a successful negotiation allows *both* sides to walk away from the table happy with the outcome. This strategy is particularly important if the negotiation involves an ongoing interaction. Here are some simple tips that can help you and your partner reach a *mutually* satisfying decision.

First and foremost, try your best to find out the concerns of your partner and don't dismiss them with unconvincing reassurances. Instead of challenging your partner, convey a sense that you are genuinely interested in your partner's objections because you want her to be happy with the decision.

Back to Kim and Carl. When asked to talk about his concerns, Carl said, "I love the energy of the city. Moving out would feel like going back home to the Midwest. It's true the Midwest was a great place to grow up, but I've become a real city person. It's not that we take advantage of the opportunities in the city every day, but I just like knowing it's all there. And it seems that our friends who have moved to the suburbs come to the city less and less as their kids get older. Also, I hate to waste so much time commuting. I will be the one who does most of the commuting and I'll have to leave the house really early, maybe even before the kids wake up, and I won't be home until late. I feel as if we'd be living separate lives and that bothers me."

In response, many people would say, "You are being selfish and thinking more about yourself than the children." This would *not* move the process along yet it is exactly the kind of thing many couples say when they are trying to change each other's position. And, of course, who doesn't become defensive and attack back when they feel assaulted?

Instead Kim said, "I understand what you're saying, and those are real concerns. Let me tell you what I'm worried about and maybe we can figure something out. I'm bothered that the kids won't have any freedom in the city. And I'm concerned about the public schools, and the competitive environment the kids will face if they have to go to private school. Space is important to me. You know how frazzled I get when everything is disorganized and cluttered. Honestly, I think I'd be calmer if I had more space. The mess of two kids running around would not bother me as much if we could keep their stuff in the family room. Also I think I would cook more if takeout food weren't so easy to get."

Second, remember that for big decisions you will need to have several conversations, in which new concerns will emerge over time. Don't be annoyed if your partner comes up with new objections and negative feelings. Good negotiations take time.

For instance, in a later conversation Carl focuses on how much time he would have to devote to upkeep of the house. Since he knows how to do all kinds of repairs himself he can't see hiring someone else to do them, but he dreads the idea of spending his weekends repairing the roof and plugging up leaky pipes. As it is now, he hardly has any time for the things he likes to do.

Kim has more concerns about living in the city. She knows that the crime rate has gone down, but recently she's heard of a number of kids being mugged by other kids right outside their schools. She knows that she's a worrier and feels that she'd worry more about the kids if they tried to raise them in the city.

Third, and most important of all, think of these differences as an opportunity to find creative solutions that will give each of you the majority of what you want. Conflicts are best resolved when you find a solution that neither of you thought of originally but that will satisfy both of your tastes and preferences. Often this idea will only arise after much thoughtful discussion.

The Third Alternative Versus Compromise

There are two ways for couples to resolve differences: either compromising or finding a third, mutually agreeable alternative. Both approaches require some creative thinking to be effective.

Compromise involves taking turns, so that for instance on one vacation your partner will do what you prefer and on another vacation you will do what he wants to do. This can be a good solution if you don't use it too frequently and if neither person has to accept things that he or she has strong negative feelings about. Think creatively about ways to help your partner enjoy your preference. And, of course, in order for this solution to work, both people need to be genuine good sports. Getting what you want is no fun if your partner participates but acts truly miserable or even halfhearted about it.

Finding a third alternative that will satisfy both you and your partner is a better way to resolve differences that have an ongoing effect on each person's life. For instance if Kim agreed to live in the city and Carl found a second job to earn more money, the agreement would probably lead to resentment and marital tension. *On important issues, a third alternative is a much better choice than compromise.*

A third alternative must incorporate the various elements that go into both you and your partner's preferences. Most conflicts that seem insurmountable come from the mistaken assumption that only one thing will make each person happy. As we have seen with Carl and Kim, if you do not treat each other as adversaries you will find that some aspects of what your partner prefers appeal to you, too. This awareness leads to third solutions that will please both people.

Kim and Carl finally decided to buy a house in a condominium development so that Carl would not be responsible for upkeep of the house. The house, though much larger than their city apartment, was considerably smaller than what Kim had hoped for, but Carl could walk to the train station and his commute was only forty minutes door to door. The development had a large common play area for the children and good local schools. They agreed to buy subscriptions to plays and concerts both for themselves and the children so that they would have to keep going into the city.

Kim was a little disappointed because this was not her dream house, but she wanted Carl to be happy and it pleased her when he immediately began planning the layout of his new study. Carl, like Kim, was not entirely happy with the decision, but the short commute and the fact that he could walk to the train station made a big difference in how he felt about leaving the city. And knowing that Kim and the kids would be happy there meant a lot, too.

Persnickety Piggery's Wise Solution

When my children were young, my husband and I loved a children's book in which various animals vie for the biggest piece of cake.[3] The pig's logic for why she should get the largest piece struck us as eminently sensible: "I should get the most because I like it the most." Persnickety Piggery's Wise Solution will help you and your partner resolve many conflicts. When you have a stalemate, the person who cares most about the issue gets to make the decision. In order for this to work, each of you has to be honest about how much you genuinely care about the issue. For instance, if one person regularly reads home furnishing books and has taken courses in interior design, it would make sense to give that person a greater say in the decision about how to arrange a room. It is not because she is an "expert," but simply because she cares more than her partner does. Persnickety Piggery's approach would mean, for instance, that the musician in the family would prevail in a conflict about where the speakers are placed, the amateur painter would decide how the pictures are hung, and the person most invested in cooking would make the final decision between the two models of stoves that the couple considers purchasing. But in order for this to work well, the less-interested partner's preferences have to be given serious consideration and the decision should not be one that the less-interested party would find really hard to live with.

Remember that treating your partner like an adversary instead of a friend will lead to a stalemate and chip away at the love and trust that are the foundation of the relationship. So when you find yourself in an argument about something and one of you says, "I don't know why you have to be part of every decision," or "You never care about [blank] except when I'm about to make a choice," or "It's not fair, it really matters a lot more to me than to you," or "Why can't you let me decide? You know it really doesn't matter as much to you," step back and think about what your partner is saying. Often there is a lot of truth in these kinds of statements. Though of course you each have some interest in the topic at hand, it may very well matter more to one of you than to the other.

The Importance of Letting Each Person March to His Own Drummer

Like most couples, as Andrea and Ronald began to fall in love with one another they were struck by their similarities. Although they had very different temperaments—Andrea was much more social and outgoing than Ronald—they loved the same movies, bands, TV shows, and even candy bars! And on a deeper level, they felt that they shared the same values and dreams.

Andrea's warm and outgoing family embraced Ronald and brought out a side to him that he really enjoyed. He had always felt somewhat awkward in groups of people and envied those he knew who had a large circle of family and friends.

Often on weekends they drove upstate to Andrea's parents' country house. The main activity was just hanging out—and often watching TV—with the steady flow of neighbors, friends, and family who were drawn to this warm, welcoming household. Ronald's family lived in California and he got to see them just once or twice a year. He missed his family and it felt good to be "adopted" by Andrea's parents.

In this day and age when so many people come from families where there has been a divorce, Andrea and Ronald were struck by another similarity. Both sets of parents had been married for over thirty years and none of their siblings, aunts, uncles, or cousins had ever been divorced.

According to Andrea, her parents were very compatible and did almost everything together. "When Mom goes shopping, Dad will go along and wait for her in the car. They are both fanatical bridge players, and although they get mad at each other a lot when they play, they wouldn't think of playing separately. Dad loves golf and Mom is now taking lessons so that she can play with him. They even cook together. To me that's what marriage is about. Doing things together."

Ronald had a similar image of married life. His dad had recently retired and now was home every day with his mom. "I know that's supposed to create a lot of trouble, but my parents seem to be doing great with so much time together. They're getting along better than they ever did. They have some separate activities—my dad likes gardening and my mom hates it—but mostly they're like Andrea's parents. They do almost everything together."

We were discussing this because Ronald and Andrea, just three years into their marriage, were on the verge of divorce. They fought about everything. While at the beginning of their relationship they seemed to like so many of the same things, they now felt as if they were extremely different and had constant arguments over how to spend free time. Ronald was annoyed that they spent so many weekends with Andrea's family. He still thought her family was wonderful, but he felt bored with the conversation and how they spent their time when they visited. And Andrea in turn felt bored and out of it when they would get together with Ronald's intellectual friends. She read current bestsellers, "not Proust," and thought that Ronald's friends looked down on her. Andrea felt hurt when Ronald wanted to do things without her, and Ronald felt guilty about doing so. They both assumed that a good marriage was one in which there was a great deal of togetherness.

In the couples counseling sessions they realized that despite their differences, which they now saw more clearly, they still felt very close to each other. Each thought the other was a really good person and potentially a terrific parent. When they weren't hurt and angry, they could be incredibly supportive of one another. "I have a lot of friends—some that go back to kindergarten—but Ronald's the one I want to talk to when I'm upset about something," said Andrea. Ronald had similar feelings: "Andrea's really the only person that I ever open up to all the way. I'm a private person, but I do talk to her—less than I used to since she's angry at me so often. I've even cried about things in front of her. She really knows how to bring me out of my shell. I trust her. It's just that we are so different and I feel that I lose too much of myself when I'm with her. We spend the evenings watching TV and then I feel like I've just wasted my time. But if I go in the bedroom to read or work on the computer, Andrea feels hurt and isolated."

Like Andrea and Ronald, many of the couples I see are disappointed, hurt, and irritated if they are out of synch with their partner. When their partner is away for a weekend, they are struck by how good it feels to do what they want. Being able to stay up late, go out for a run early in the morning, eat different kinds of foods—all sorts of activities are greatly affected by the desires of one's partner. Expecting too much accommodation and coordination gets many couples into trouble. If one person is doing more accommodating than the other, a well of resentment can build up and unexpectedly erupt. After years of seeming to get along, one person may become overwhelmed with the feeling of having given up his or her identity.

This is what happened to Ronald. He believed that he might need to leave the relationship to get his identity back. He felt that he hardly read anymore, saw very little of his friends, and hadn't played chess in years. As Ronald began to feel that he was losing himself in the relationship he did try to assert himself more. This led to arguments, stalemates, and hurt feelings. He wanted

Andrea to do more of what *he* wanted and she felt pressured to be someone she felt she wasn't.

Though of course some couples have more in common than others and don't have to negotiate so often, many couples do have quite different interests and tastes. This isn't a problem if both partners feel comfortable doing things separately and do not interpret it as a failure or lack of connectedness.

Many couples I work with are helped by the suggestion that they simply accept the dissimilarities and find ways in the structure of their lives to incorporate different preferences. For instance, Ronald might still go with Andrea to her parents' house but not quite so often. And when he came with her, Andrea could encourage him to go into another room to work or read if he felt like it rather than being sociable for the entire visit.

Andrea would need to accept more separateness in the evenings since Ronald wanted to watch less TV. If she felt lonely she could use this time for catch-up phone calls with her many friends. Rather than nagging Andrea to read books that she had no interest in, Ronald decided to join a friend's book group so that he would have people with whom he could discuss his more esoteric reading.

The point here is that *people sometimes need to march to their own drummer*. A morning person who likes getting out early in the day will become irritable if he can't go out until his partner is ready. And a night person who loves the quiet hours of solitude at one or two A.M. will feel a real loss if she always goes to bed at eleven P.M.

But how do you know how much separateness is okay? Wouldn't it be better to be with someone who has more in common with you? Wouldn't Ronald just be settling when he could find someone more compatible? Especially if the couple doesn't have children, do they really have to be so separate for each of them to get what he or she wants? These are tough questions, and frankly I think they should be tough. Even when children aren't involved, breaking up a relationship is serious and shouldn't be done simply because the grass may look greener somewhere else. There's a lot to be said for commitment, history, and stability. Chapter 6 will offer you some guidelines for deciding whether there is enough good in the relationship to stay committed to one another. In my experience, when a couple allows each other more autonomy the gratifying parts of the relationship become more obvious and closeness returns.

What about when there are kids in the picture and you want to have some family time? Maintaining a balance between separateness and togetherness is more difficult when the couple faces time constraints, whether it's children, a job that requires a lot of traveling, or incompatible work schedules. It is often very difficult to figure out how to manage to be an "I," a couple, and a family. These complex issues will be discussed again from somewhat different angles in both chapters 6 and 7.

For now, you might be able to resolve many of the types of difficulties described in this chapter simply by accepting your differences and finding ways for each of you to have it your way.

The strategies described earlier will resolve many of the differences that were described in the beginning of the chapter. For instance, the couple who had different tastes in furniture might be able to resolve the stalemate by using Persnickety Piggery's Wise Solution. Perhaps furniture design really is more important to one partner, and with an attitude of cooperation and goodwill the problem can be solved. If each person really dislikes the other's preferred furniture, perhaps there is a third alternative that—though not a first choice of either—is liked well enough by the other. So instead of antique pine or modern, the couple can agree on Shaker-style furniture. They are each compensated by knowing that their partner is happy, too.

Over and over again I see couples who have been stuck in their differences for years rapidly find solutions once they start thinking about these issues in a new way. However, no strategy will work unless you remember the most important point of the chapter. *There will never be a real winner if you treat each other like adversaries or if you are too cautious about joining.* No strategy can replace an attitude of goodwill and a wish to see your partner happy. Solutions come more easily and angry struggles turn into opportunities for creative brainstorming when you remember that you are on the same side.

Chapter 3

We Love Each Other, But . . .
We Get into Really Bad Arguments

Since I do a lot of relatively short-term couples counseling, I generally have room in my schedule to start with one new couple each week. In preparation for writing this chapter, I reviewed notes from the last twenty consultations. In around half of these cases the couples said in essence that they got along well until a fight erupted.

- Thirty-one-year-old Charles said, "I'm scared by what happens when we get into an argument. Isabel sobs hysterically, and it goes on all night. We have to stop this. I hate it."

- Francine, age forty-five and in her second marriage, said, "I can't take it anymore. I need stability. It's a real roller coaster. When Mark and I aren't fighting we have a great relationship. Then I say or do something that sets him off and he just goes wild. He screams and curses at me, and then after he cools off he expects me to act like nothing happened. After a while I do forget about it, but it's beginning to take its toll on me. I feel like I'm walking on eggshells around him."

- Charlotte, in a committed relationship with Stephanie for more than ten years, felt that their awful fights contributed to her depression. "Everyone tells us that we are great together, and I think our relationship can be terrific, but then something will happen to make us so angry with each other that I think we both feel we shouldn't be together. Stephanie becomes extremely cold, and I can't take living in that kind of icy atmosphere. We talk, scream, and talk some more, but nothing gets resolved."

- Janice, who has been seeing Martin for over two years, was apprehensive about getting married. She felt that they really loved one another but they still had terrible fights. "Martin behaves in a hurtful way, and he just doesn't see it," she says. When she tries to explain to him how he's hurt her, she only gets more frustrated. "He always says that I'm misinterpreting things. He never admits to anything, and he makes me feel like I'm really crazy for reacting this way. When we're not in this kind of tangle, he can be so sensitive and caring." She worries about whether they should get married when they argue so frequently. She's concerned about raising children in such an unstable relationship.

- Robert, who has been seriously involved with Becky for three years, said, "We have to find a way to stop these arguments, or as much as we love each other I think we'll have to separate. I'm getting scared. Our fights have become physical and I hate myself for hitting her. I can't believe I've become someone who would resort to force. I try to walk away from her when I feel enraged, but she grabs me and insists that we talk. When she's in my face like that I lose control. I know it's terrible, and I swear I never acted this way before. The weird thing is that aside from our violent arguments I really think this is the best relationship I've ever been in. Nutty, huh?"

- Jeremy, after living with Jonathon for more than five years, could no longer tolerate how nasty Jonathon became when they fought. Jeremy and Jonathon grew up in vastly different environments. Nobody ever speaks harshly in Jeremy's family, whereas in Jonathon's they yell and scream at each other. Jeremy felt demeaned by Jonathon's shouting and couldn't get through to him that this type of behavior was unacceptable. He threatened to leave Jonathon many times, but the good things about their relationship prevented him from ever taking this final step.

All these couples are in relationships that work well in many ways, but when there is a disagreement, as there is bound to be even in the best of relationships, things spin out of control. In this chapter I describe ways to discuss difficult issues that minimize escalations and arguments. I give you five tips for getting through to your spouse and five tips for listening to complaints so that you can avoid frustrating, irrational, and depressing arguments. These simple steps will enable you to hear each other better, but *first you need to learn to de-escalate while you learn and practice new ways to communicate.*

Learning to De-escalate

It takes time, practice, and patience to master new ways of communicating, and you may find yourself in the middle of an escalation even before you finish this chapter. Once an argument starts to escalate you no longer hear one another, and it is pointless to continue trying to make yourself understood. These arguments never end well. Usually both parties feel extremely frustrated and lose hope that their partner will ever acknowledge and accept their point of view. For days or even weeks after an escalation, you and your partner may feel alienated from each other. You may be depressed or seething with anger. You may feel completely misunderstood and emotionally isolated. And worse still, such arguments can reach a physical or abusive level out of sheer frustration.

Many couples that I work with minimize the importance of the physical aspect of their fighting. Often the person who has been abused doesn't mention it, primarily to avoid humiliating his or her partner by talking about it candidly. Some people minimize the violence because they feel shame for remaining in an abusive relationship. Often the one who has been assaulted minimizes the incident because he or she feels guilty for "provoking" it. Even if physical force occurs infrequently, it has serious consequences and must be controlled. *Fear in a relationship is not conducive to love and intimacy.*

The following steps for preventing escalations apply to those disagreements that lead to violence as well as to other intense arguments. But if you are currently in a relationship where hitting, shoving, shaking, scratching, pinching, slapping, or punching occurs regularly, you should seek professional help even if no one is actually hurt by the violence. The strategies that follow will call a halt to these "arguments from hell," even if the issues that you argue about do not get resolved entirely.

Step #1: Establishing a STOP Rule
You must agree that if either one of you feels the familiar futility of an argument spiraling out of control, that person will call a halt to the argument. Either one of you can call a cease-fire. Often, one person in the interaction will think that they are engaged in a *discussion*—not an argument—that it is important to have then and there. This should not override the STOP rule. Only one of you has to feel uncomfortable with this argument to invoke the

STOP rule. Keep a written copy of this STOP rule on an index card in a place where you will see it frequently. Many people like the idea of keeping the rule in a sock or underwear drawer, since it's a private place that you see every day. The rule should simply say: *We each agree to respect the other's wish to stop the discussion, even if one of us does not think it is an escalating argument.*

Step #2: Learn to Recognize When a Disagreement Is Escalating into a Bad Argument

You probably already have a sense of when a discussion will turn into an argument. Here are some of the signs:

- Are you thinking, "Oh, no, here we go again!"?
- Do you have a sinking feeling that you are entering an area where you have extreme differences of opinion and where previous discussions have never led to a meeting of the minds?
- Do you feel as if you are going around in circles?
- Is the argument getting so entangled that you're not even sure what each of you is talking about anymore?
- Are one or both of you starting to say very hurtful things?

These are signs that the disagreement has escalated, and one of you should exercise your option to call a halt to the argument.

Step #3: Disengage and Allow Your Partner to Withdraw

It's not easy to stop midstream, especially when you believe that you are on the verge of making yourself understood. It can be very frustrating when your partner says he doesn't want to continue the discussion any longer.

You may feel upset that he is avoiding your justifiable anger, but it's important to remind yourself that it will not be productive to continue to "discuss" something when your partner thinks things are escalating. We will address further what to do if you feel your spouse avoids conflicts. But for now it is important for each of you to recognize the signs of destructive arguments and stop the interaction when either one of you feels uncomfortable. If your partner says something like, "I don't want to talk about it anymore," "I've got to get out of here," or "This is going nowhere," you must find a way to postpone the discussion until a time when you will be able to talk about it in a more productive manner.

Plan in advance what you will do to calm down when stopped midstream. In my work with patients I always ask them to think about what has calmed them down in the past or lifted their moods when they were upset. Asking yourself this question in advance can be surprisingly beneficial. Often people haven't given much thought to what helps them regain their emotional equilibrium, but with a little effort almost everyone can think of something.

Some people feel that they shouldn't distract themselves when they are upset. This type of thinking does not help. In fact, the ability to distract ourselves allows us to control our feelings rather than let our feelings control us.

So ask yourself what works well for you. Would it help you to write down what you weren't able to finish saying? Does being alone for a while calm you down? Does listening to music change your mood? Working at the computer? Cooking? Watching TV? Reading? Even cleaning a closet might help when you need to disengage from a bad argument. Of course, if you have children you might not be able to be by yourself. So think of some activities that you can do while you watch the children, such as painting or drawing with them, playing ball, or helping them with homework. Many people find it helpful to call a close friend or relative. But think ahead of time about who is a calming influence. Which of your friends helps you keep things in perspective?

Write down these calming activities and keep the list in an easily accessible place so that when you are upset you don't forget what will get your mind off the argument.

Remember the positive feelings you have for your partner. You will be able to disengage from an escalating argument more easily if you remember that only yesterday you felt very close to this person at whom you now feel enraged. Many people have a difficult time holding on to a picture of the whole person when they are angry. Some people use the psychological mechanism of "splitting": a person is either all good or all bad. Instead of recognizing your partner as someone you love who is making you very angry at the moment, splitting leads you to forget the good feelings that are present most of the time. Instead you experience him only as bad, mean, and uncaring. Splitting causes you to feel only love or only hate, without integrating the feelings into a more complex and realistic whole. When angry you tend to wonder if you do love him or if you ever have loved him.

If, when angry, you consciously try to think of close moments, these frightening and confusing feelings will most likely fade. People have more control over their thoughts than they realize. You can refocus your thoughts from thinking that you don't really love him to remembering times when he was supportive and caring. From your memory bank you can pull out the feeling of closeness during sex, or when you are cuddled up watching TV together, or when you peal with laughter over a private joke, or when you look forward to a Saturday night out together. If you tend to split off positive feelings when you are angry, you will be surprised by how readily they can come back if you make the conscious effort to recall positives. And you will find that having this perspective will help you to calm down more easily.

Calm down by physically withdrawing from each other. If you and your partner have a history of getting into arguments that become physical, it is important to establish spaces that each of you can retreat to, knowing that this place is off-limits for your spouse.

Leaving the house is usually not necessary if you know that some part of your home will be your temporary sanctuary. You each need to agree not to pursue the other into that space.

- No banging on doors.
- No talking through doors or windows.
- No slipping notes under doors.

Think this location through in advance and write it down as part of the agreement, which you will keep where you can see it every day.

Step #4: Set a Date to Talk about the Issue Again

Many people have difficulty walking away from an argument. Intensely involved in the issue at that moment, they don't want to sweep it under the carpet. For this reason, make a point of setting a definite time that you and your partner will revisit the problem. In my experience, the argument will start up again if you talk about it while you are still stinging from the hurtful words that have been said. *Let at least twenty-four hours pass before you confront the issues again.* The more time passes, the easier it will be to approach the disagreement in a productive manner.

Most important:

Step #5: When You Call a Halt to the Argument, You Each Must Honestly Agree to Consider the Other's Point of View

Saying and meaning that you will give thought to what has been said helps put the argument behind you. I can't emphasize enough that you must be absolutely sincere about your willingness to give thought to what your partner has been saying. You must agree to acknowledge your partner's perspective and try to put yourself in his or her shoes. If you have done this, you will find that when you return to the discussion a day or two later, each of you will have something different to say and you are more likely to find a common meeting ground. If you follow this one tip, you will be well on your way to a more harmonious relationship.

Now that I have covered what I think of as relationship first aid, here are some tips to help you express your concerns in a way that will not only decrease the chance of escalations but also help you get through to each other.

Five Tips on How to Talk About What Is Bothering You

- "I just can't get through to him," said Abby. "Sometimes I'm embarrassed by how rude he is to waiters and service people but when I try to talk to him about it he blows up at me."
- "She doesn't pay any attention to what I want," said Arty. "Over and over again I ask her to please get rid of the junk

that is taking over the house. I can't stand the clutter, but she continues to collect things and refuses to throw anything out."

- Beth told me, "I don't believe him anymore when he promises he'll be home early. I'm really fed up. There's always an excuse for why he had to stay later. And even when he calls to tell me he's leaving and will be home in half an hour, he's not home for an hour and a half."
- Sarah feels that it's impossible to tear her husband away from the children. When she wants to get a baby-sitter, he says he feels bad going out without them. He never wants to go out alone with her.

Everyone in a relationship has experienced something similar to what these people describe. We all have times when we can't get through to our partner or make him understand how we feel. And we all sometimes feel intensely frustrated and angry, even furious, at our spouse. This experience leads to the type of escalations described in the beginning of the chapter.

Here are some simple tips that have helped countless couples to talk in a way that encourages their partner to listen. These tips are not foolproof. They will not solve all your difficulties. But in my experience they help enormously and can lead to real changes in behavior and attitude.

Tip #1: Talk about Difficult Subjects When You Feel Close to Your Partner, *Not* When You Are Angry

When your husband comes home late again after promising to be home early, of course you are angry. Venting your anger at that time may be satisfying, especially if you manage to extract an apology and a promise from him that he will try harder in the future. Yet you know from past experience that his promises are short-lived, leading you to be even more incensed the next time it happens.

If instead you discussed the issue at a time when you were not as angry and he was not as defensive, you would be more likely to get through to him. Couples counseling can be so effective because a good couples therapist enables both people to talk about what bothers them without simply venting anger at their partner. In the calm atmosphere of a therapist's office couples can discuss difficult topics without the flow of adrenaline, allowing each to more genuinely consider the other's point of view.

Most people respond to anger by being defensive. Even if your partner is one of the rare people who can apologize (more will be said about apologies shortly), he or she probably won't fully listen to your concerns when they are expressed in a very angry manner. When anger is directed at people, all sorts of emotions are stirred up that interfere with the ability to hear and have empathy for the other's point of view.

Feeling attacked, many people attack back. Even if Beth's continually late husband knows that her anger is justified, he may instinctively fight back and say something like, "You don't understand anything about my work—you're too spoiled." Once that occurs, a productive discussion is almost impossible!

Most people have a strong impulse to avoid anger. Hundreds of times I've heard people comment, "I just can't take his/her anger." Some people who have this reaction do the equivalent of children who cover their ears with their hands when they don't want to hear you. They let you vent, don't say much, and hope the storm will pass.

Wanting the anger to disappear quickly leads some people to make conciliatory promises that they will not really keep. Although they are sincere when they make these promises, the desire to appease and reduce the anger motivates their behavior instead of a well-thought-out decision.

When couples make promises during a therapy session I always ask the person who is promising to make sure he feels comfortable with the commitment. I urge him to discuss his reservations so that they can come to realistic agreements. It is best to avoid making promises while in the middle of an argument. And if a promise *is* made, consider it provisional, not final and irrevocable.

In chapter 5 we will talk more about how to control your anger. For now, just remind yourself that getting angry at your partner has only worked in the short-term and hasn't really resolved the problem.

When you are angry you could say, "You know I'm upset, but I think it would be better to talk about the issue at some other time when I'm not feeling so mad." You must then let go of your anger and relate to your partner in a normal and friendly manner.

Most people don't want to bring up difficult issues when things are going well, because they fear that it will lead to an argument, which will then ruin the warm and close feeling they are now enjoying. This is a valid concern and certainly one of you can ruin the good times by throwing a monkey wrench into your developing closeness. However, if you follow the rest of these tips the discussion will not lead to an argument. Instead you will each feel understood and perhaps even closer to one another.

Obtain your partner's consent before you introduce uncomfortable issues again. Saying, "I'd like to talk with you about something serious for ten minutes or so—is that okay?" will usually elicit a positive response.

Tip #2: Talk About What Pleases You, Not Only About What Bothers You

Many people do not accept criticism well, and often interpret it in an exaggerated way. They feel worthless and rejected by their partner.

Dena, for instance, was devastated when Elaine told her that she felt constrained by Dena's reluctance to go out whenever she felt a little sick. She wished Dena wouldn't focus so much on every ache and pain and take to bed as soon as she didn't feel well. This criticism made Dena feel like Elaine didn't love her anymore and wasn't happy in the relationship.

Similar reactions can occur when your partner overgeneralizes from your criticism. Criticism leads people to become defensive, excessively conciliatory, angry, or so hurt and depressed that a productive discussion can't occur.

Even if your partner does not respond to criticism as if it were a denouncement of her whole being, it still helps to preface negative statements with positive ones that let your partner know you have not forgotten her good qualities. If, for instance, Elaine said, "Dena, you know how close I feel to you most of the time, but it really bothers me when . . ." Dena might have listened to Elaine's concerns without being so devastated.

In the case in which the husband continues to be late despite his promises, the wife could preface her criticism with "I know that you have good intentions when you say you will be home early and that you really do want to see the kids before they go to bed, but it's a real problem for me when you don't come home when you've said you would."

Do not think of positive statements as part of a strategy or a manipulation. Including a comment on your partner's good qualities allows *both* of you to keep the problem in perspective. By remembering the whole person, the angry person is a bit less angry and the criticized person is less defensive.

Tip #3: Shorter Is Better

This means both that you should speak in short paragraphs and that you should try hard to keep the total exchange to no more than fifteen or twenty minutes.

Speak in short paragraphs. Some people ramble on and on and expect their partner to listen without interruption. Although this may be okay once in a while when you have to get your point out all at once, generally it does not lend itself to a productive discussion.

When one person talks in long paragraphs without pausing, the other person tends to feel impatient waiting to respond. After a couple of minutes, he stops listening receptively because he is trying to hold on to his thoughts until he has an opportunity to reply.

Another important reason to talk in short paragraphs is that most people feel controlled and trapped when someone expects them to listen without responding. When one person does most of the talking, the other sometimes feels like a child who is being reprimanded for a misdeed.

Limit the total length of the discussion to fifteen or twenty minutes. Frequently I hear people say that they dread discussing problems because once they start, the discussion continues endlessly without going anywhere. "I get a knot in my stomach when I hear my wife say she wants to talk to me about something," says Ed. "Once it starts I might as well kiss the rest of the afternoon good-bye. I resent not only what she is saying, but that we have to waste the whole day arguing." If your partner feels this way it is even more important to promise to limit the time spent on a discussion to no more than fifteen minutes. You will accomplish more in those fifteen minutes than in a two-hour debate. Your partner will be more relaxed and willing to listen if he knows that you don't intend to spend the whole afternoon or evening rehashing your position.

One trick to keeping it short is to stop the discussion when you sense that you are getting nowhere. Don't persist in trying to get through to your partner. Instead you should agree to put the conversation on hold with the understanding that you'll each give real thought to the other's point of view.

Tip #4: Stick to the Point and Don't Revisit Old Hurts

This is probably the most difficult and "unnatural" tip you will find in this book, but it is also one of the most important.

For most of us, once we start talking about one thing that bothers us we inevitably link that thing to other things. Although this is a natural impulse, your partner will feel barraged by your complaints. Instead of really considering your point he will shut down. He may begin to feel that he can never please you. The more you resist the temptation to let one complaint flow into another, the better. It helps to remember that you will dilute the power and effectiveness of what you say if it becomes one of many points rather than the central focus.

Try to notice when you are on a roll—when you have the feeling of "letting it all out" or when you hear yourself say, "And another thing that bothers me is when . . ." You will also know you are on a roll when you start talking about your partner's character—using terms like "your hostility," "your passivity," "your lack of compassion," or "your lack of consideration for others." These types of global character attacks will take you down a hurtful and unproductive path. Comments like these are experienced as a condemnation of the whole person and they lead to anger and defensiveness.

If you focus on specific actions and behaviors that your partner can actually change, you are more likely to be heard. For instance, saying "It bothers me when you forget that I'm anxious about a doctor's appointment and don't ask me anything about it," is quite different from saying "You're not nurturant" and then going through a list of the ways your partner has failed to come through for you.

And finally, *do not revisit old hurts and injuries that have been discussed many times before.*

- "Can't you ever let go of that?"
- "Here we go again!"
- "Am I going to have to pay forever for a mistake I made years ago?"
- "I thought things were good, and now you bring up that again!"
- "I feel hopeless. No matter what I do you keep going back to that."
- "I'm *sick* of hearing about this—what's wrong with you? Can't you forget it?"
- "*Nothing's* ever finished with you."
- "Nothing's ever forgotten—you have a memory like an elephant."
- "I've said I'm sorry *over and over* again. What do you want from me?"

These statements are typical reactions when one partner, hoping to illustrate or reinforce a point, brings up events that may have occurred years ago. Often you no longer feel angry or hurt by the old incident, but you think it will help your partner understand what is now bothering you. But going back for any reason is usually so upsetting to the "guilty" party that whatever point you were trying to make goes unnoticed.

Tip #5: Be Careful What You Say—Harmful Words Can't Be Taken Back

People say all sorts of things when they are angry that they do not actually mean, and later show surprise when their partner has taken the hurtful words so seriously. Even if you apologize and explain that you didn't mean what you said, your partner may still be hurt. She may think that what you have said in anger reflects what you *really* feel deep down. Harsh words may be forgiven, consciously forgotten, and dismissed, but they may still linger in the heart and soul of your mate.

Your partner not only feels wounded by your words but by the fact that you wanted to be so hurtful. I have heard many people say that they get upset by how mean their partner gets when they are angry. It is extremely distressing to know that a person you love and who loves you can enjoy hurting you so much.

"I know he was very angry but it really makes me wonder if he loves me when he is so intent on putting a knife in my heart with his words. How can you love someone and want to hurt them that way? I just don't understand," said Emma, who had forgiven her husband but was still disturbed by what happened.

Certainly it is possible to love someone and still want to cause them pain. When angry, people tend to forget the whole person and for the moment see their partner only as someone bad who has hurt them and whom they wish to hurt back. But no matter how angry you feel toward your partner, try to remember that most of the time you love this person.

Five Tips for How to Listen to Complaints So That a Productive Discussion Occurs, Rather Than an Argument

Many people have a hard time listening nondefensively to their partner's dissatisfactions. You or your partner may be sensitive to criticism no matter how nicely it is couched. People often respond to complaints as if they were devastating attacks. Feeling attacked, they counter the criticism with complaints of their own. Learning to really listen to your partner's complaints instead of reacting is a key element in avoiding escalating arguments. These tips will help you and your partner listen to one another even when the criticism hurts you. And often, when you really listen rather than react emotionally, you will find that your partner's complaint is not so bad and you will feel less hurt.

Tip #1: Listen for What You Can Understand and Not for What You Disagree With

I can generally tell by the look in their eyes when someone is listening to their partner only in order to figure out how to rebut and hit the ball back into their partner's (who is at the moment their opponent) court. When I see this happening I say, "The key to making this a productive experience is to *listen* differently than you ordinarily do. Most people listen to their partner's complaints or criticisms with the mind-set of trying to refute, correct, and prove that their partner is wrong. If instead you listen with the attitude of trying to understand the general point being made, even if the specifics aren't quite correct, you will find that these discussions really will help you work things out. Listening with the intention of trying hard to "get it," even if your partner isn't accurate, will go a long way in helping to resolve your conflicts.

So when your partner talks to you about something that upsets him, try to focus *not* on the wrong or incorrect parts, but rather on the parts of the statement that you can agree with or even "sort of" understand. By consciously responding to what you *can* understand, acknowledge, and accept, you take a giant step toward having a productive conversation rather than a debate. Your partner will notice that you are really trying to understand his concerns. He will feel validated and understood to some degree. And even if you can agree with only one small part of what he has said, the experience of being understood and affirmed creates goodwill and changes the whole tone of the interaction.

Here is an example of what I mean by listening for what you can agree with:

Francine: "I feel like you don't really *think* about me most of the time. It's like you still think of yourself as an individual and not part of a couple. Even the way you say 'I saw that movie' when we are out with people, rather than 'We saw that movie.' Or, 'I want to go to Australia one of these days' instead of 'We're hoping to go to Australia.' It's peculiar and it makes me feel weird—almost as if you forget that we are a couple. And when you come home late, or forget something from the store that I asked you to bring home, or watch TV alone in the living room all night, I feel like you don't think about me or want to be with me."

George, with whom Francine has lived for the past four years, could disagree with a lot of what she has said. For instance,

George might feel that Francine has wrongly interpreted the meaning of his forgetting to bring things home from the store, getting home late, or watching TV at night. Many explanations for these behaviors have nothing to do with not thinking about Francine, and if George responds to that part of the statement, a debate and unproductive argument will most certainly follow.

But George realizes that Francine's comments about his use of "I" and not "we" does ring true. Instead of telling Francine that she is wrong about the meaning of watching TV, George could say, "I guess it *is* a little odd that I say 'I' when I mean 'we.' I don't really think it means that I don't think about you, but I can understand how it feels that way to you. I'll try not to do it. Maybe it does show that I have trouble thinking of myself as a couple. I didn't think so, but I see how it's strange. Let me think about this couple versus individual business. Maybe there is something to what you're saying."

George can then say something about not agreeing with the other points, and Francine, who we hope is also listening for what she can agree with, will be more inclined to understand George's point of view because she feels that her main point has been seriously considered.

Tip #2: Don't Counterpunch: The Importance of Timing and Context

Do not respond to your partner's complaint with a complaint of your own. Here's an example of what I mean:

> GAYLE: I'm very upset about something. Can we talk about it now for a few minutes?
>
> HANK: Okay, but I have to leave in fifteen minutes. What's bothering you?
>
> GAYLE: I feel as if you think that the house and kids are

my responsibility, even though my job is just as demanding as yours. You do help out, but I have to *ask* you to do everything. You don't assume the kids are your responsibility, too. It really bothers me. I know you take care of a lot of things, but I still think the division of labor is unfair. If one of the kids is sick I'm the one who has to find a baby-sitter or stay home from work if I can't find one. You never think of taking time off.

HANK: Well, I'm bothered by things you do, too—I just don't complain about them! It makes me mad that you spend so much time on the phone with your sister and your girlfriends. The phone rings all night and I don't know why you have to speak to them every day. You're barely home for ten minutes when you start talking to your sister! If you want to start complaining, I have a lot of stuff that I could complain about myself.

GAYLE: Why haven't you raised it before? Why did you wait until now to bring it up? You're just digging up something to get off the topic.

HANK: No, it really bothers me. It's always bothered me. You'd rather talk to your sister than to me. I think you're too attached to her and the time you spend talking to her could be spent with the kids, who have been waiting to see you all day.

GAYLE: *You're* telling *me* about time away from the kids!? I don't believe it! Once again you've turned my complaint into a discussion about what's wrong with *me!* I'm too attached to my sister! I'm not a good mother! How come it's always about me and never about you? I'm really sick of this. It happens every time I try to talk to you about something that's bothering me. It always becomes something about what's bothering you.

The escalation in this conversation is almost inevitable when the response to criticism is countercriticism. Although Hank might have some real concerns, he should raise them at another time so that they can be dealt with as an independent issue.

Escalations occur when the person with a complaint feels unheard and unacknowledged. No matter how genuine Hank's concerns are, by raising them in response to Gayle's criticism he turns the focus to *his* concerns, and Gayle understandably feels frustrated and dismissed.

You will avoid those painfully circular accusations and counteraccusations that go nowhere, if you stick to one person's complaints at a time. If your partner does respond with a counterpunch, it will help if you acknowledge the concern and set a definite time to talk about the issue he raised.

Tip #3: Stay Focused on the Main Point, Not on Irrelevant Details

Remember when you were a kid learning reading comprehension? You had to find the subject sentence and determine the main point of the paragraph. Many people forget this skill when they are in the midst of an emotionally charged conversation. Helping couples focus on the main point in a discussion is one of the most important aspects of my work. Often one person will pick up on and respond to a minor point within what the other has said. When this happens, the discussion loses all focus and the couple talks *at*, not *to*, each other.

Here are some examples of off-point and on-point responses:

HELEN: Let me give you an example of what's bothering me. Remember when I had that accident last month in the snowstorm? I was upset that you seemed more concerned about what had happened to the car than to me. When you picked me up at the service station you didn't even ask me if I was okay. I felt as if you didn't even care about how I was feeling. I forget what you were doing when I called, shoveling snow or something—which is pretty risky to do at your age. Anyway, I really felt like I was just a nuisance to you and that you were more annoyed than worried. And when you came in, you went into the bedroom and didn't talk to me all evening. You were withdrawn and angry. All because of the car.

IVAN: I've told you a million times that *it's perfectly okay for me to shovel snow!* I did what you asked—I had a stress test and it was fine!

Ivan's response is off-point. Though Helen does mention something about being unhappy with his snow-shoveling, it is clearly an aside for her. The main point—that she felt uncared about because of Ivan's concern about the damage to the car—was not responded to. And to make matters worse, Helen then responds to Ivan's off-point response, and before you know it the argument becomes so convoluted that neither of them even remembers what it was about in the first place.

HELEN: It makes me so mad how macho you are about your health!

IVAN: You think anyone who doesn't think exactly like you is crazy. You always think you know what's right. You have an opinion on everything.

Eventually when I encouraged Ivan to focus on the main point, Helen's hurt feelings, here's what he said:

"I wasn't worried because I saw right away that you were all right. I know you think I don't worry about you enough or act 'nurturant.' But I'm different from you. I don't talk about what I feel, I just *do* things. Like when I bought you a cell phone even though you didn't think you needed it. But you're right, I was angry that day. The accident happened because you made a left turn without looking carefully, and I've told you over and over again that you have to be more careful! You're going to get yourself killed one of these days! I felt like yelling at you, but knew I shouldn't because you were upset, so I just decided the best bet was for me to keep my distance."

This response addresses Helen's statement directly.

Ivan's original statement occurred because he felt criticized and then responded with a counterattack. Had Helen prefaced her statement by saying "I know you love me and that you do a lot of very caring things, but on the day of the accident I felt that . . ." Ivan probably would have responded to the main point right away.

Here are a few more examples of off-point and on-point responses:

> ROBERT: I feel like our whole lifestyle rests on my shoulders. It's hard for me to go to work every morning and see you lounging around the house reading the paper. You've been out of work now for over eight months, and I don't feel like you're doing much about it. I think you could be doing a lot more to find a job. You act as if money isn't an issue. Well, it is. We have no money put away for a rainy day, much less retirement. I pay all the bills. I figure out who has to be paid right now and who we can put off for a while. And you just spend, spend, spend, without giving it any thought. You act like money grows on trees. You're always talking about wanting a new car, wanting to move to a bigger house, wanting to go on vacation. Vacation from what!? You're on

vacation all the time, as far as I can see! I feel as if I'm the grown-up and you're the child!

JEROME: You're the grown-up! That's a laugh! You're afraid of your own shadow! I have to make *every* phone call. I arrange our whole social life. You're too scared to ask our neighbor if we can borrow his lawn mower when ours is broken. I can't believe you think I'm the child and you're the grown-up!

Robert's main point—his concern about money and resentment about Jerome's "irresponsible" attitude—was not addressed. Often people respond to an irrelevant detail because some highly charged words have been spoken. In chapter 5 we will talk about knowing and avoiding the "hot spots" or "fighting words" that really affect your partner. For Jerome, being called childish had a particular sting to it. Furthermore, Robert presented his worries about money in an attacking manner and Jerome picked up on a statement that he could use as part of his defense.

Here's one last example:

JAYNE: I feel as if you tune out when I'm talking to you— you look at magazines instead of at me. You seem as if you're hardly listening, and can't wait until I stop talking and leave you alone. You do the same thing with the kids, and you make promises to them that you don't keep. I think it's because you don't even *listen* to what they're saying in the first place and just say yes without knowing what you're agreeing to.

KEN: You're the one who says yes to them all the time, not me. You spoil them. I couldn't believe you told Matt we would consider getting him a car when he turned seventeen.

Ken picked up on a subpoint rather than addressing Jayne's main concern—that she feels Ken tunes her out. It's not that Ken's concerns are invalid. It's simply that as discussed in Tip #2, when a complaint made by one person turns into an opportunity for the *other* person to voice complaints, the first person feels frustrated, ignored, and unacknowledged. So when you and your partner seem to be going around in circles, stop for a moment and ask yourself the main point of the first statement made.

In the above example, Jerome might say to Robert, "I'm sorry you feel burdened by the money situation. But I *am* trying hard to find a job. What else do you think I should be doing? Where do you want me to cut back in spending? I think you're panicking. I think you have an anxiety about money and most of the time you're aware of it yourself. I'm not saying anything that you don't already know!"

Or Ken might have said to Jayne, "I disagree with what you're saying about not really paying attention. You know I can glance at a magazine and pay attention at the same time. I think you're oversensitive about this. You have this thing about having my full attention. It's unrealistic."

These examples show that staying on target is not the same as *agreeing* with what has been said. But it is a step in the direction of reaching resolution. Ken disagrees with Jayne, and Jerome disagrees with Robert, but at least they are talking about the same topic, so that there is a chance of working it out.

Learn how to hear the main point. It's not always easy to hear the main point. Your partner may throw a lot at you at once or say things that really push your buttons. Or you may have been sitting on a lot of your own complaints and feel like saying, "If you think you're the only one with complaints, let me tell you about it!" If you just say anything that you feel like in response to your partner's complaints, you will probably find yourself in one of those awful, endless, and escalating arguments. Try to stick to the main point initially presented even if it seems unfair and difficult to do.

The best way to ensure that you stick to the main point is to check in with your partner and ask, "Is your point that you feel I don't care about you?" (Helen and Ivan) or "Are you worried that I'm not holding up my end of things financially?" (Jerome and Robert), or "Do you think I tune you out and find your talking annoying?" (Jayne and Ken).

If your partner says, "Yes, that's right," then you can go ahead with the conversation. If instead you hear, "No, that's not what I mean," ask your partner to elaborate. You may have to remind him or her to keep the paragraphs short and not to get on a roll.

Tip #4: Don't Play Psychologist

- "I don't think this is really about me. You're acting as if I'm your mother. I can't ask you to do anything without you feeling *controlled*. It's all about your mother. *She's* controlling, not me."
- "You're in a bad mood because you didn't get that job and you're just taking it out on me."
- "You're oversensitive. Other people would know that I'm joking but you interpret every joke as a hostile comment."
- "You like to bury your head in the sand just like your father. That's why you're angry at me. You hate to hear the truth."
- "You're being passive-aggressive. You can't express your hostility directly."
- "This is PMS. Don't you keep track of your cycles? I do this all the time and it doesn't bother you—it's just that time of the month."

When said in response to your partner's criticism, these types of comments will almost always lead to an escalating argument. Even if there is some truth to what you are saying, it cannot be absorbed when your partner is trying to tell you about something that bothers her.

Convincing people that psychological processes affect their feelings and behavior is difficult under the best of circumstances. People experience "interpretations" of this sort as attacks. Rather than leading people to think about the truth, they only intensify anger and the feeling of being misunderstood.

Sometimes during moments of closeness and trust you may be able to say these things without your partner becoming defensive. Even this, however, is unlikely. In chapter 5 you will learn how to deal with each other's emotional baggage without trying to convince your partner that his reactions are unwarranted.

Tip #5: Don't Beat a Dead Horse—Try to Give Honest Thought to Your Partner's Point of View

If you and your partner are unable to come to an agreement, it is not productive to continue on and on with the argument. You need to find a way to end the discussion without either of you feeling hopeless about ever getting through to the other.

The following has worked for the hundreds of couples I have counseled: You must each agree to give serious, honest thought to the other person's point of view and to get back to each other on the issues after you have given them some thought. For this to be effective, make a commitment to consider a *specific* point, not, "I'll think about what you have said."

So, for instance, Ken might say to Jayne, "I'll think about whether sometimes I do just wish you would stop talking. I don't think that's true, but I'll think about it and try to notice when it's happening." Jerome might say, "I'll think about whether I'm overreacting, and I'll take a look at our finances more closely to see if you're right. But you need to think about what I'm saying, too. I still think you could look for a job with more energy than you do." If each person follows through on their commitment, giving real thought to the other's point of view, the next discussion will be a more productive one.

In chapter 7 we will discuss the importance of each person changing even when the other is not doing it equally. So even if your partner has not followed the tips for talking about problems in a way that makes them easier to hear, do not use it as an excuse for not following the Good Listening Tips yourself.

A Word About Apologies

Many people long for apologies. Being apologized to and having the other party acknowledge how they have hurt you can be very gratifying. It is the stuff of romance. We have witnessed the scene of the contrite lover begging forgiveness over and over again in romantic fiction and movies. Unfortunately these sorts of apologies *are* largely the stuff of fiction.

Some people crave apologies for another reason. They desperately need to have their hurts acknowledged because they were disregarded when they were growing up. Perhaps no one ever acknowledged that there were events and interactions going on in their home that damaged them emotionally. They may have been made to feel crazy for their feelings and were told that nothing bad was really happening. For these people, an apology is not about romance. It is about having their hurts taken seriously. They have a strong need for their partner to accept responsibility for his actions and to affirm that they had real reason to feel harmed.

When that happens, it is almost like a childhood fantasy has come true—a fantasy in which parents or siblings who have been hurtful see the injustice of their actions and ask forgiveness. If you or your spouse has had that kind of experience in childhood, there is bound to be some emotional baggage. In chapter 5 we will look at how to deal with emotional baggage in a relationship.

Although the wish for an apology is both understandable and often warranted, it can prolong conflict and lead to lasting bad feelings in a relationship. Couples tend to get bogged down in the issue of apologies because the apology serves as an admission of guilt. The "wronged" party wants the other to accept total responsibility for what has occurred and sees himself largely as the victim of the other's misconduct. Although on some occasions one person is entirely in the wrong and the other is entirely in the right, this one-sided view is seldom accurate. Most, although again not all, hurtful events involve two people behaving in relation to each other. If an apology means that the hurt party bears no responsibility for what happened, then often the partner will not want to apologize.

"It's always just *me*. You never acknowledge *your* part in what happened. I'm always the bad guy and you're perfect," said Zach, in response to Wendy's statement that she couldn't get over what happened until Zach came through with a *real* apology.

"You owe *me* an apology, too, then," he continued. "You acted just as bad as I did. Even though we have spent hours talking about what happened, the bottom line is that you still believe it was my fault. There's no use in talking about things— it always comes down to the fact that it's my fault we had an argument. I wasn't nice enough. Or sensitive enough. Or considerate enough. Or I should apologize for my tone of voice.

Or the look on my face. I'm not going to apologize. It's ridiculous!"

These reactions will lead to intense escalations or feelings of futility when discussing events. Why was Zach so hostile and angry about being asked to apologize? The answer is that he really believed that the argument was not entirely his fault. If Wendy had acknowledged her part in what happened and then asked for an apology, she would have had a greater chance at success.

Often people try to extend a partial apology that doesn't conflict with their belief that they are not completely to blame for the argument. "I'm sorry that I upset you," "I'm sorry that you felt hurt by what I said," "I regret having said that," "I wish I hadn't responded to you the way I did," or "I didn't mean to hurt you" are the type of statements that are often offered by way of apology because they do not say, "I'm terrible. I did something awful. It's all my fault. Please forgive me."

When at all possible, accept these statements as apologies. You may not feel totally satisfied, but for you to get satisfaction may mean that your partner has to be humiliated or filled with self-recriminations. Ask yourself if you really want this from the person you love and whether such feelings will lead to closeness. Thinking about the effect it will have on your partner may help you to let go of the wish for an admission of complete, unequivocal responsibility.

Demanding an apology can be harmful. Your partner may feel as if he or she is being asked to grovel. There is something humiliating about being forced to apologize on demand. It can make the apologizer feel like a child or like someone lacking in self-respect.

Last but not least, *heartfelt apologies offered spontaneously and voluntarily can go a long way toward warming your partner's heart.* Ask yourself if this is one of those situations where you really were in the wrong and it doesn't make sense to talk about your partner's part in the problem. If that is the case, then it is important to acknowledge it, since it will only insult and infuriate your partner to insist on a mutual contribution to a one-sided problem.

• • •

This chapter has been filled with advice that if followed will help you avoid most horrible arguments. Do not get discouraged if you still have some bad arguments. Most couples do have bad run-ins from time to time, but if you use these tips they should happen much less frequently.

And remember to be forgiving of yourself and your partner. Try as you might, neither of you will follow all of the tips described here. Don't get discouraged. Don't get critical of yourself or your partner for doing it all wrong. Just keep at it and you will eventually see a change in the intensity and duration of the arguments. Don't expect perfection. As the psychoanalyst Harry Stack Sullivan so wisely said, "We are all more simply human than otherwise." And isn't that what love is all about?

Chapter 4

We Love Each Other, But . . . We Don't Have Much of a Sex Life

Many couples who get along well, and feel close to each other in many ways, don't have sex—at least not very often. For some couples who don't have sex regularly, it's really not a problem. Each of them feels comfortable with the state of their sex life.

Even if a couple isn't having sex at all, I don't assume when counseling them that they are unhappy about it. There are no laws that say a couple must have sex. If you and your partner are not having sex, it's important to assess if you are *really* upset about it or if you simply feel you *should* be doing it, and that's why you feel upset?

Certainly, I believe that for most couples connecting sexually is an important part of a relationship. Having a good sex life doesn't solve all of a couple's problems, but for many it is like the grease that keeps a machine running smoothly. It doesn't prevent them from having fights, being disappointed in each other, or feeling that the chores are distributed unfairly, but it *does* provide a sense of connectedness that helps them put their complaints about each other in perspective. Many couples report that when they do have sex they feel more relaxed with one another for days afterward. Somehow things just go more smoothly.

Some couples are physically close to one another, but not in a sexual way. They may cuddle a lot, watch TV snuggled up with one another, sleep together like spoons, or lie tangled all night like pretzels. This physical closeness connects them like glue even when other aspects of the relationship are not going very well. Because of their physical intimacy, they don't feel as if they are living together only as friends. For some couples this is enough, but many people who are physically close in this way still feel disappointed that there is no sex in their lives. They may not think about it much or get frustrated by its absence, but they feel bad because they know it's one of the pleasures of being human that they're not experiencing.

Even if you are content with having little sex in your relationship, this chapter can help if your partner feels disappointed or frustrated about your sex life. Sometimes one person in a couple feels satisfied with the relationship even though there is little or no sex. As far as he is concerned they are at a point in their lives when other things are much more important. But if it upsets one of you then it is bound to have an impact on the relationship, and some solutions must be found.

Sean and Jane had been together for over fifteen years and it had been more than five years since they had had sex. Sean didn't seem to care about sex at all anymore but Jane still did. Jane was angry—not because they weren't having sex, but because she felt that Sean didn't seem to care about her needs and wasn't interested in making things better between them. It is a big source of tension for many couples when one of them calls it quits regarding sex without considering how his or her partner feels about having a nonsexual relationship. Many, like Jane, feel angry. Others feel hurt and unloved.

"I don't understand it," says Manny, who has been married to Judith for eight years. "She says she loves me, and I guess she does. But how come she doesn't care about my need to have sex? I know she's been depressed lately—the last couple of years have been hard because her mom has been sick—but doesn't she care about what I'm feeling? At thirty-eight I'm not ready to be put out to pasture yet! She acts as if I'm being mean to her if I ask her just to try and see what happens. 'You know I can't help it,' she says. 'You know I'm just not interested—I'm too stressed. What if I had an illness and couldn't have sex? Would you be mad about that, too?' I'm mad and hurt but I end up feeling guilty. She could try to please me even if she's not in the mood herself. I really feel as if in some deep way she doesn't care about me. If she did, she'd at least make some effort."

Many people dismiss their spouse's concerns and even get angry because their partner's dissatisfaction makes them feel guilty and inadequate. In short, they become defensive about the problem rather than address it. The defensiveness comes not only from feelings of guilt and inadequacy, but also from the mistaken belief that nothing can be done about a lack of desire or a low sex drive.

Even when two people have sex regularly, one of them may feel that his or her partner doesn't have much of a sex drive anymore. The most common concern I hear from couples is not about *bad sex*, but about *not enough interest in sex*.

Here are some of the statements I've heard in my office in recent months:

- "When we do have sex, it's fine, but then weeks can go by and nothing happens between us," says thirty-four-year-old David. "I don't understand it. If it's so good, why don't we seem to want it more often? I'm not blaming my wife, though sometimes I do feel that she gives off signals that she's not interested, which kind of kills any ideas I have about starting something. I just sense her lack of interest and get turned off."

- "I know he's a lot easier to live with when we've had sex," says Jamie. "But I'm just not interested most of the time and it feels like a chore to do it just to keep him happy."

- In a private session with me Eleanor says, "I don't want to hurt Frank's feelings, but I just don't feel much passion anymore. I don't know if it's me or him. When I look at him I see a middle-aged guy with a paunch and I just don't have much desire. But I can't say I'm turned on by anyone else, either. When we have sex I do get into it, but I never initiate it because I really don't feel attracted to him anymore. To be honest, I'm not sure if I ever did."

- "What's normal, Doc?" asks Joe. "Is it normal for a couple our age (thirty-one and thirty-five) to have sex just once a week? Am I expecting too much? Tell me honestly. I'd like to have sex every night, but I know she will get mad if I push it. But, jeez . . . I'm too young to live like this. I really *need* some release. I'm not kidding. Is the problem me or her? She doesn't seem to care if weeks go by."

- "Gregory and I are very physical with each other," says Margie. "We cuddle a lot and sleep like spoons. But when I try to do more I get rejected. I don't even try anymore. It just leads to a fight."

- "My sex drive seems to be gone," says Lisa. "Ever since the baby was born I just don't feel like having sex anymore. I never thought this would happen to me, but I'm really not interested."

- "He tries to make me feel guilty for his own frustration, and that makes me even less willing," says Rita. "My sex drive isn't as strong as his, and it makes me mad that he won't accept that."

What to Do When You've Lost Interest in Sex

For many if not most people, interest in sex decreases dramatically after a few years in a relationship. Familiarity definitely affects sexual desire. The intensity of desire during the early stages of a relationship is just not sustainable. Newness and romance are powerful aphrodisiacs.

Faced with a decrease in spontaneous desire, many people just put the whole business on the back burner. They don't think much about sex. It's not that desire is gone entirely; often sex is quite good once the couple actually gets started. It's as if their sexual being has gone into hibernation, but can and does reawaken from time to time. Sometimes, even after a good sexual experience together sexual desire goes into hibernation once again.

With some conscious effort, you can keep sexual desire alive and combat the natural lack of desire that comes with familiarity. Here's how.

Tip #1: Make Sexual Contact a Part of Your Daily Life in Small but Definitely Erotic Ways

A large part of why familiarity leads to the lessening of sexual desire is that so many of your interactions in a long-term relationship have absolutely nothing to do with being lovers. Most of the time you and your spouse probably act like partners who are running the enterprise of home and family together. During the day-to-day running of your life, it's easy to forget what goes on between you in bed. It's almost as if you are two separate sets of people and the one in the bedroom has nothing to do with the one who clears the table, paints the house, pays bills, calls the plumber, helps the kids with homework, weeds the garden, and tries once again to make sense of a checkbook that just won't reconcile!

Yet when you were lovers just starting out, your sexual beings were a part of you no matter what you were doing. Remember the feeling of not being able to keep your hands off each other? Perhaps you would come up behind your boyfriend while he was on a business call and kiss the back of his neck. Or maybe he would call you at work and say something about what happened in bed the night before that made you blush. Or you would nibble at his ear while he was reading the newspaper. And sometimes you acted like teenagers while driving to work together. Do you remember screaming, "Keep your hands on the wheel!" or "Stop, they'll see us!" All that touching and fooling around came spontaneously in those days. Your passion for one another just couldn't be boxed away and taken out only in bed.

Here's the key: *Even if you do the same types of things consciously rather than spontaneously, they will still have a powerful effect on your relationship and keep you feeling sexy.* Each little bit of erotic contact you have with each other throughout the day keeps your sexual self from going into hibernation. And because these teasing behaviors occur at times when you couldn't possibly have sex, they are even more titillating. If while you're driving to work you gently rub your hand up and down your partner's thigh, you make it much harder for each of you to forget that you are still lovers, not just partners. And though you may not actually get together for sex for several days, the little bits of sexual arousal accumulate in a long, slow tease that makes the coming together more intense when it eventually does happen.

When it comes to sexual desire, the less you are aroused the less you want it. By being stimulated in small ways almost daily, you will preserve your appetite for sex. When there is little sexual contact you get used to scarcity, so to speak. It's like being on a diet. Most people report that their cravings for certain foods disappear over time when they have gone for a while without them. As many people know, when it comes to eating or drinking, it's often harder to have just a little of something than to have none at all. Fooling around a little bit is like having a small taste of something, and like the taste of forbidden foods it makes you want to have more.

How not to get rebuffed. Many people complain that when they try to tease and fool around they get rejected. Frequently I hear statements like these:

- "When I grab her in the kitchen, she pulls away as if I'm bothering her."
- "He always makes advances at the wrong time. We're supposed to leave the house in fifteen minutes, and he starts up. What does he expect? Of course he's going to get shot down!"
- "The kids are around, and he's trying to get me into the bedroom. They're going to burst in, and he knows it. I think he *wants* me to reject him. He *knows* that they don't pay any attention to a closed door!"
- "When I come up behind him while he's working at the computer, I feel his whole body stiffen. It seems as if he doesn't want me to bother him."

A common reason for not responding to a spouse's sexual playfulness is that "fooling around" often feels like being grabbed at rather than being touched in a truly enticing way. There's no point in touching your spouse in ways that you know from experience she doesn't like. It will only cause your partner to retreat more. If you think of these stolen moments as a chance to do something that truly arouses your partner, you will know what to do.

Many people don't respond because they feel that their partner's touching may actually be an attempt to initiate sex. A response could be construed as a willingness to go further. You are much less likely to get rebuffed if you make it clear to your partner that you're just fooling around for a minute and have no intention of pressuring him to do more.

If, you let your partner know that you are not seducing him when you rub his neck while he's working at the computer, he's much more likely to relax and enjoy it. The stolen kiss or touch when the kids are nearby will probably be well-received if you make it clear to your partner that you know you can't really do anything now and are just fooling around a little.

Some people say that this type of teasing is impossible because their partner becomes aroused so quickly that putting actual sex on hold until later is too frustrating. Generally this is more a matter of attitude than arousal. We all know how to calm ourselves if we want or need to do so. But if your partner has trouble with the degree of arousal that occurs when you fool around, then you need to tone down the teasing.

Tip #2: When You Have Sexual Contact with Your Partner, Make a Conscious Effort to Let the Experience Linger in Your Memory

Again, let's take a look at what tends to happen naturally in the beginning stages of a relationship. Many people report that they think about the sexual contact they had with their partner long after it's over. Do you remember sitting at a meeting and having a momentary memory of some delicious sensation from the night before? Or perhaps before falling asleep you imagine the touch and feel of your lover's body against your own. Although these memories occurred on their own when the relationship was new and the sexual feeling between you was intense, you can also intentionally recall them. You will help prevent your sex drive from going into a deep freeze if you make a point of calling up memories of pleasurable sexual experiences you have had with your partner. By doing this, you make the sexual contact last well beyond the actual time it took place.

The next morning when you are lying in bed trying to get up, let your mind drift back for a minute toward what felt good the night before. Or perhaps as you daydream on the train to work you can picture the things you did to each other in bed the prior evening. You will see if you try that this is quite easy to do. All you have to do is *remember to remember*. This will help you keep the very private intimacy that exists between you and your partner in the forefront of your consciousness. So even though you may both rush out in the morning and come home to children needing help with homework, you will not so easily forget that your relationship extends beyond running a household together.

You can also bring an awareness of the bedroom into your everyday life by *mentally* caressing your partner while watching him go about his everyday activities. At one time or another you've probably imagined kissing or touching someone you found attractive. Again, you can do consciously what sometimes occurs spontaneously. For instance, when your husband is sitting on the couch watching a basketball game, or reading a story to one of the kids, or talking on the phone to his mother, see if you can visualize him as the same man you were making love to just a few nights before. Perhaps you will picture yourself running your hand down his chest, gently stroking his face, or kissing his eyelids. Try visualizing yourself touching him in the ways you make love. This simple mental exercise should take no more than half a minute. It will feel like a momentary daydream that you snap out of almost immediately. Yet brief as it is, it will serve as an important reminder that you and your partner have a sexual intimacy that is always there despite day-to-day activities and chores.

Tip #3: Stop, Look, and Listen

One way to stay aware of your sexual self is simply to pay attention to things that you would find arousing if you let yourself really look at them. Sexual images surround us all. People who have put their sexuality in hibernation see but don't really attend to the stimulating sexual messages that bombard us all the time. One simple way to keep yourself feeling in the mood for sexual contact is to let your eyes linger for a moment on the latest Calvin Klein advertisement or Victoria's Secret catalog. You may think you already notice these things all the time. But do you look closely, or do you flip the pages quickly, barely glancing at what you might find stimulating?

Some people feel almost as if it is cheating to actually seek out sexual stimulation to jump-start their sex drive. They feel as if they should just be in the mood naturally or get turned on only by their partner. And of course, some people do feel sexually aroused without having to make any particular effort to awaken sexual interest. But for many, the daily demands of job and family life make it difficult for sexual arousal to occur "naturally." I have seen many couples benefit from simply accepting that it was okay for one or both of them to use sexually explicit material to get them in the mood for sex with their partner. Many people are offended, however, if they feel that their partner is using pornographic material to get aroused.

In recent years an interesting alternative to hard-core pornography has become available. These are "teaching" tapes that show normal-looking couples of all shapes and sizes engaged in all sorts of sexual behavior. It's like being able to peek into the bedroom of the couple next door and watch them, which many couples find exciting. Every bit as explicit as X-rated videos, many people find them not only more morally acceptable but also more arousing. Unlike most pornography, they portray people with whom couples can readily identify. The couple treats each other with respect and tenderness. Body parts are of normal size and there are no larger-than-life, depersonalized, or degrading scenes. The tapes are narrated by sex therapists and provide information and education about how to stimulate and satisfy your partner in a large variety of ways. Some couples are comfortable watching these tapes together while others are okay with one or both of them watching privately.

If you feel that your sex drive has seriously diminished you can help it come back by doing things that whet your appetite. You may find that you prefer erotic literature to watching videos, or that plain old romantic comedies turn you on. Whatever it is, *do it*. Although it may seem unnatural, it is just as unnatural to let your sexuality disappear.

Tip #4: Enjoy Your Own Body

Enjoying your own body is crucial to feeling sexy. Even if you feel overweight or too thin, or that your breasts are too large or too small, or you have a middle-aged paunch, you probably have moments when you can forget about your "defects" and get into a state of mind where you relax and enjoy the feel of your body. We openly talk about singing in the shower, but for many people a lot of other good stuff goes on behind the plastic curtain! So with soap on your hands, and the privacy to enter into a sensual mindset, see if you can let yourself enjoy the roundness of your belly or the fullness of your breasts. The more you take pleasure in your body, the less likely your sexual self will go into hibernation.

Music as an aphrodisiac. Music can be a powerful aphrodisiac. Dancing to the right music can transform you from someone who feels draggy and overburdened with chores, to a lighthearted, light-footed, sexy, sensual, juiced-up woman. Music loosens us up and brings out the sexy self hidden in most of us. Some music seems to naturally call for hip-swaying and suggestive gyrations! People on a dance floor forget about their size and shape. No matter what your chronological age, dancing makes you feel young. You can (and probably sometimes already do) have that same experience when you are alone in your house listening to music. Alone you can exaggerate the sexually suggestive movements as much as you like without embarrassment. You can run your hands down your body or perform an imaginary striptease. The more you follow the little inklings of sexuality you feel, the more your drive will increase. If you have danced in front of the mirror early in the evening you are more likely to be in the mood later that evening in bed. And, of course, dancing with your partner in your bedroom is an excellent way for both of you to get in the mood—assuming that you are not one of the many couples who get into fights when dancing!

Tip #5: Have Sex Even If You Think You Are Not Interested

Waiting until you're in the mood to have sex is probably the most common reason that couples begin to lose interest. Chores, kids, exhaustion, and job stress are not exactly conducive to wanting sex. If you're like most people who constantly juggle multiple demands, relaxed and romantic moments are few and far between. Waiting for the right mood causes problems because, as we have seen, the less you have sex, the less you want it. So if you find time for a romantic evening only once every month or two, your sexual self will become less and less powerful. If instead you just make it part of what you do on a regular basis, regardless of whether you are actually in the mood, you will prevent your sexuality from going into cold storage.

Use sexual contact to get *in the mood.* Most people who have been with each other for a long time only occasionally feel spontaneously aroused by each other. But this sense of familiarity also has its benefits. After years of being together, you probably have become experts on the places and types of touch that you each find most enjoyable. Even if you don't feel in the mood at first, after a short time you'll probably get turned on. Below I will discuss what to do if you *can't* get into it. But most often, if you decide to have sex you will find that it works out pretty well. Sometimes it will turn into something very passionate, and other times it will simply be a quickie, or as one couple called it, a "Hello, how are you?" kind of sex. If you think of sex as something you do on a regular basis whether or not you are in the mood, you will find that more and more you *will* be in the mood.

But you may be thinking, "I just can't relax or change gears that quickly," or "I'm so tired at the end of the day that I'll fall asleep in two minutes if I get into bed," or "I need some time for myself at the end of the evening." All these feelings are valid and there is no point in forcing yourself to have sex if you're going to resent it. You don't have to have sex on a regular schedule or whenever your partner wants to, but if you adopt the attitude of "I'll try and see what happens," you will have a more active sex life than if you wait until you feel in the mood.

Being out of Sync

If you follow the tips described above, soon you will feel more sexually alive. But for many couples, the problem is not a sleepy sex drive but finding the time to get together.

"We really seem to be out of sync," says twenty-nine-year-old Caroline, with despair and frustration in her voice. "In the morning, when *I'm* interested, *he's* not, and at night, when *he* wants to, I feel like all *I* want to do is go to sleep. He thinks I'm into some kind of power struggle but I really am tired at night. And he definitely isn't a morning person! Since the baby gave up napping a couple of months ago, there is literally no time during the day. It's really depressing."

There are no easy answers to this problem. But if you have the "I'll give it a try" attitude discussed in Tip #5, you'll find more overlap and time for you to get together. For instance, Caroline might be up for having sex right after putting the baby down, even if she would be more in the mood in the morning. And perhaps her husband might give it a try in the morning, with the thought that he'll probably get into it anyway.

Scheduled Sex

Pairing the words *schedule* and *sex* sends chills down the spines of many couples. "Please, hear me out," I say when I see a frown as I start to talk about it. With the right attitude, planning not only helps ensure that sex happens but also makes the sexual experience more intense. Planning can mean anything from saying after dinner, "How about if we meet in bed at 9:30 tonight?" to marking an evening on your calendar that you reserve for spending intimate time together.

Frequently couples find that once they overcome the idea that sex should be spontaneous, planning works very well. With free time so scarce most people mentally plan out their schedules pretty carefully, and many people dislike being taken off-course even for sex. Perhaps you had been looking forward to watching a particular TV show, finishing the mystery you were reading, clearing up the mess on your desk, or cooking something for the next day's party. Although you know it's not warranted, you may feel annoyed when your partner tries to initiate something spontaneously. The irritation you feel at shifting gears can lead to hostility and blame when the real reason you're angry is because you're overscheduled. If you or your partner think you have a problem with shifting gears, then it almost certainly helps to plan when you will get together for intimate physical contact.

Planned "dates" also have the advantage of allowing for the pleasure of anticipation. Remember when you were new lovers? You knew that after dinner you'd be going back to your house to make love. Perhaps you were a bit excited all day, knowing that you were going to be together that evening. You thought about what to wear to look and feel sexy. You set out flowers, chose a nice wine, and put your favorite CD on the stereo. When you and your partner have a date for lovemaking, all this is possible. And though it's not the same as when you were new to one another, you can still make it a special event. You could plan a picnic dinner in bed, or a gourmet feast to precede or follow lovemaking, or a special movie that you will watch together as part of the evening. Or you might simply want to shower, use a special cologne, or take a luxurious bath using bath oils you've saved for a special occasion.

"Uh-oh," you may be thinking. "Doesn't this put a lot of pressure on us? It turns the event into such a big deal that we'll have performance anxiety!" This could certainly happen unless you make sure that you both understand this risk. But being sexually intimate will be good for your relationship regardless of whether or not what happens between you is terrific or just so-so. If one of you has trouble getting aroused, just relax and enjoy the sense of closeness that can come from stroking and caressing one another. Your attitude should be, "Let's set aside this time to be with one another, and we'll see where it goes." It's crucial that you really mean this and that it is not just a superficial attempt to take the pressure off the situation. An attitude of acceptance and flexibility will make your date a positive experience.

When Sex with Your Partner Doesn't Feel Right

Ginger wanted to speak to me privately because she didn't want to hurt her husband's feelings. "Nothing I'm about to tell you is a secret," she said, "but it's hard to talk about it in front of him. It's not that I'm not interested in sex. I often feel aroused and I masturbate a lot. It's just that it doesn't work with him. It's not only that I don't have an orgasm. That alone wouldn't be so much of a problem, because if I was frustrated I think we'd both be okay if I made myself come. The real problem is that I really don't like having sex with him. He touches me in all the wrong places. I feel completely uninterested when we make love. I think about the shopping list or what I have to do the next day at work. I feel detached and unresponsive. Pete can tell, and he keeps trying harder to turn me on, but nothing he does works. In fact, the more he tries, the more annoyed I feel. I know he's struggling, but I feel so irritated with him. His touch is too gentle and he has the wrong rhythm. He's like a bad dancer in bed. He moves too slowly and when I'm finally beginning to enjoy it he stops what he's doing and tries something else. And he never seems to pick up on what I *don't* like, either. He kisses me on the neck even though I've told him many times that I feel ticklish there. That really makes me mad! Why does he keep doing something that I don't like?"

Ginger, thirty-two, and Pete, thirty-four, had been married three years. They had no children, and Ginger wondered if they should stay together, because their sex life just didn't work. "I feel as if I'm too young to resign myself to this kind of sex, but we do really well together in so many other ways. He's my best friend—I tell him everything. But when it comes to sex he gets defensive, stubborn, and mad at me if I say something. I keep asking myself, how important is it, anyway? Why can't I be less irritated by it? And why can't he learn? I feel so confused. What worries me is that I find myself drawn to a man at work whom I know would love to get me into bed. But I know that if I start fooling around, I'm really calling it quits on the marriage." Ginger asked if they could do anything about their lack of compatibility, or if it is one of those things that either is or isn't there.

When I spoke to Pete about their sex life, he agreed that they have a real problem. But he felt that Ginger had some hang-ups from things that happened in her childhood, which made it hard for her to relax. "She can't give up control," he said. "That's why nothing I do is quite right—she'd rather do it herself. I try, but no matter what I do, she's not happy. I'm reluctant to try anymore. What's the point? She ends up frustrated and mad and I feel bad because I can't please her. Basically she's telling me that I stink as a lover. I've had other relationships where women didn't feel that way."

The story of Ginger and Pete is a familiar one. In fact, I've heard variations of it many times. For instance:

- Jackie likes sex to be forceful and a bit rough. Her partner, Ronnie, enjoys slow, gentle sex. They feel annoyed at each other and find that when they do have sex they often end up in an argument.

- Margaret doesn't like receiving oral sex. Lee finds this upsetting, because for Lee, giving oral sex is an important part of lovemaking and without it sex feels empty.

- Charles and Stacy have different tastes when it comes to kissing. For Charles, kissing is one of the most arousing, sexy things that a couple can do. But for Stacy, kissing is not the least bit erotic.

- Keith complains that Marcia is so particular about what she does and doesn't like that he has no room to be spontaneous. "I feel like I'm servicing her, not making love to her. I can arouse her if I hold to the script, but it feels like I'm just following a program. Insert part A into part B. To tell you the truth, I find sex boring. She does good stuff to me, but the feeling that I'm just going through a set routine takes away from it."

- Gloria worries because in order to get turned on she has to fantasize about something else. She would never want to act out her fantasies, and she feels ashamed and disturbed by them.

- "He always wants sex and it makes me mad," says Cleo. "It

doesn't feel like it's about me—desiring *me* or loving *me*. I could be anyone. He has a need and I'm supposed to satisfy it."

- Stuart complains that Laura is too fastidious. Before Laura will have sex, Stuart must shower, brush his teeth, and put on cologne. This annoys Stuart because it means that sex can't be spontaneous and it makes him feel that his natural self must be repulsive to her.

- "We have good sex, I guess, but it doesn't feel like making love," says Olga. "It's intense, but not gentle and loving. We never lie around and talk afterward. We do it and then we go to sleep."

How to Resolve These Differences

Let's go back to Ginger and Pete to see how we worked on these issues in couples therapy. Many of the solutions are things that you and your spouse can easily do on your own.

The first step is to make a sincere effort to understand how your partner feels so that you stop blaming one another. With a spirit of cooperation and a commitment to making the other happy, you can do many things to get more in synch. As we talked about how Ginger felt that Pete's rhythm was off, I asked Pete to try hard to understand what his wife meant. Pete came to understand it as something like the frustration of having his back scratched by someone who never quite hit the right spot. "Go down a little. No, up a little more. Now slightly to the left," are not meant to be controlling, but simply to get the itch scratched in a way that feels good.

Pete also could relate it to masturbating. He pretty much did it the same way all the time with the pressure and rhythm that worked for him. Thinking about his own need for the right touch and rhythm helped Pete feel much less angry at Ginger. If you, like Pete, can find something in your own life that is similar to what your partner describes, it enables you to substitute empathy for anger.

Ginger also needed to understand why Pete felt useless trying to please her. She realized that her frustration had caused her to lash out at him, and she apologized for making him feel it was his fault that they happened to have a different sense of timing and rhythm. She acknowledged that some other woman might find his timing and touch just right.

Learning to have the right touch and rhythm. "Even if you don't have the natural chemistry that you each have had with others, you *can* learn to be more in sync," I told Ginger and Pete. "You can learn to be good in bed, just as you can learn to dance together even if you started out stumbling over each other's feet. Since you both agree that except for sex you have a good relationship, it would be a shame to break up over a lack of natural chemistry." Both nodded in enthusiastic agreement. Their marriage felt at risk, and they were relieved to know that there were things they could do to solve this major problem.

An enduring sex life is based not on intense passion and chemistry but on knowing how to please each other. Many couples report that as the years go by their sex life gets better and better. Instead of familiarity leading to boredom, it can and often does lead to a comfort and know-how that makes sex very gratifying.

Ginger and Pete, like many of the couples I work with, became so entangled in hurt feelings and anger that they cut short the process of learning about each other's likes and dislikes. Once they stopped blaming each other, Ginger and Pete could make it a joint project to learn how to please each other.

Couples can learn to have the right touch and rhythm in a

number of ways. Though words can help—"A little softer," "Faster," "More pressure"—demonstrating what feels good is easier than trying to describe it in words. Many sex therapists recommend taking your partner's hand and moving it the way you like best. If you sit between your partner's legs with your back to his chest you are in a good position to take his hands and show him just what you like.

It's important for both of you to demonstrate your preferences, even if only one of you has been overtly dissatisfied. Some people simply make do even if something could be more satisfying because they don't want to complain. Not surprisingly, Pete had been overriding some of his own frustrations and it was not until doing this exercise that Ginger learned that he preferred to have her touch him more forcefully.

Some couples use sensuous massages to communicate what feels good to their partner. Giving "instructions" when getting a massage seems more acceptable than giving and getting directions during sex. But a massage is not sex. So it is important to actually work on getting the right rhythm during sex as well. Use massage as a starting ground for more intimacy.

It's important to be a good sport about your partner's directives and not to interpret them as criticisms. You may find this difficult if your spouse has a history of being critical. Hopefully, as you work together to improve your sex life you will be less blaming of one another. By taking the time to really figure out what works, each of you is investing in your future together. After a while you won't need a running commentary to get it right, but for now try to take it in stride.

It's also important to verbally communicate when you do like something, when the rhythm feels *right*, and when you'd like more of something. It's easier to accept positive input than negative feedback. Though you each must try hard not to get offended when your spouse says "Not there," or "That's too hard," or "You're tickling me," it will help if you try hard to catch the moments that are going well and instruct your partner through praise.

Another good way to show your partner what you want is to watch instructional videos together. We have already talked about using these videos to get your sex drive going, but they are also an excellent way to show each other what you would like. It's much easier to understand terms like "Go slow," "Linger," or "Really take your time," "Be more forceful," and "Be more energetic" when you can actually see what your partner means. Many people feel shy talking about what they want and find that it is easier to point out what they like in the videos.

Educating each other sexually takes time. Don't expect things to change overnight. Remember that when your partner moves his hand too quickly, is too rough, or holds you in a way that feels uncomfortable, he is doing what comes naturally. It takes time and patience to learn to substitute new behaviors for the old ones. You may find yourself feeling irritated with your partner. "How can he do it again after we've gone over and over it?" you may think. You must try to remember that he does it not out of stubbornness or stupidity, but simply because it's hard to change actions that come naturally for ones that do not. When you find yourself feeling angry and frustrated, try to remember that this is the same person who has worked hard at learning to be more in sync with you.

What to do when you have different sexual preferences. Almost every couple has to figure out what to do about the fact that their sexual tastes are never exactly the same. No matter how similar you and your partner may be, you probably have different tastes in a lot of things. You may like many of the same foods, for instance, yet have some real differences of opinion. Why then should sex be any different? It is almost inevitable that there will be sexual activities that one of you likes and the other doesn't. Unlike most of your differences, when it comes to sexual tastes each of you depends on the other's participation to get what pleases you. You can eat clams even if your partner finds them disgusting, but you can't enjoy giving or receiving oral sex if your partner won't participate. Often people feel disappointed, even when their partner willingly participates in something that he or she normally doesn't prefer, because they want their partner to enjoy it more.

Here are some ways that other couples have handled the fact that they like different things. First, expand your sexual repertoire so that you and your partner have the opportunity to find more areas of overlap. If you like only a few things that must be done in a particular order, your partner might feel that he merely "services" you. If you watch videos or read books on sex and experiment together, you will probably discover some things that you didn't know you liked and that turn on both of you. The more you explore, the more you will find mutually gratifying modes of interacting sexually. The more creative and playful you are, the more likely you will come up with a repertoire you both enjoy.

Second, take turns giving each other what each of you likes— but don't keep count. For instance, if your spouse really enjoys oral sex but it doesn't do much for you, do it anyway. And he in turn should do some things for you that are not much of a turn on for him. *However, don't do anything that you find truly unpleasant or distasteful,* because it will put a negative cast on the whole sexual interaction.

Some people have trouble accepting when their spouse does something merely to please them. They feel guilty and want their spouse to enjoy it more. You will feel less guilty if you make sure to reciprocate by doing things for your partner that you know he likes. And though it would be nice if you both liked everything equally, it's not realistic. Your partner can kiss you even if it doesn't turn him on, but you can't demand his *enjoyment*.

Sometimes, however, true enjoyment does develop with time. This can happen if you pair something that you feel neutral about with something that you find very arousing. It's a form of conditioning that often occurs naturally. So, if you're not passionate about kissing, but it takes place while your partner fondles your breasts—which does turn you on—kissing may in itself become more erotic since it's paired in your psyche with having your breasts touched. Although this transfer of erotic feeling from one region to another may happen naturally over time, it should not be consciously planned. If done in a calculated way, neither the kissing nor the fondling is likely to arouse you.

Don't worry about being distracted. Many women tell me that they have trouble clearing their mind of daily chores and responsibilities. I call this the Shopping List Syndrome. This natural and common occurrence becomes a problem only if you worry about it or take it as proof that you are not in the mood for sex. In fact it probably only means that you need a little warm-up time. Don't stop your sexual activity because you are distracted. Don't try to stop or control your thoughts. Just relax and let your thoughts go where they will. Your mind may be preoccupied but your body will respond anyway. If you stick with it you will find that after a while the pleasurable physical sensations win out and break through your obsessive thoughts.

Another common concern is that orgasm occurs only when fantasizing about some other sexual act with someone else. Although making love involves two people, orgasm itself is an entirely *individual* experience. Most people pull inward and concentrate on the intense sensation that takes them over the top. And everybody is wired for sexual arousal in his own unique and often odd way. The scenarios that many people find arousing have little to do with who they are or what they value in reality. The fact that the fantasies that bring you to orgasm have nothing to do with your partner in no way indicates that you are dissatisfied with him.

Turning sex into lovemaking. Some couples worry about a lack of closeness and feeling for one another when they have sex. "I know I shouldn't complain," says Cheryl. "After fifteen years we still seem to know how to turn each other on. We know all the right spots to touch, and amazingly enough they still work. But when we're done we get on with things as if nothing happened between us. It's just something we can do for each other—like a foot massage or something. It doesn't feel like it has anything to do with love."

Cheryl's concern is one that I have heard voiced by both men and women; men need to feel cherished and loved every bit as much as women do. For instance, when Sam complained that sex with his partner "works well, but there's nothing spontaneous about it," he made it clear that he craved sexual contact that evolved naturally from feeling close emotionally. When sex becomes simply a physical and not an emotional activity, many people feel a sense of emptiness. "Is that *it?*" asked Sam. "That's what it's all about—just getting a physical need met? I can do that myself!"

But there are some things you can do to turn sex into lovemaking. First, when you and your partner are physically intimate you need to bring the loving feelings you have for one another into the bedroom. This is not simply saying "I love you," which, though always good, is not sufficient in itself. If instead you think to yourself, "This is the person I love," and you consciously attempt to convey that feeling in the way you touch your partner, the whole experience will be suffused with love. You can convey love physically by adding tender, caressing touches to your repertoire. Stroking your loved one's brow, running your finger gently across his lips, and kissing his eyelids or her forehead will communicate your love. By combining loving thoughts with gentle, affectionate gestures, you will find that your intimate contact feels much more meaningful.

Kissing each other before, after, and during sex also helps change the experience into lovemaking. For many people, kissing is more intimate than other sexual activities. Kissing, though erotic, is also a statement of love and affection.

It also helps to spend some time together before and after sex so that the physical act occurs in a loving and attentive context. This is not possible (and probably not even desirable) all the time, but it can help turn sex into lovemaking. By adding even a minute or two of holding and kissing to a quickie, you can convert the experience into something more meaningful and romantic.

Turning lovemaking into just plain sex. Many people feel that everything has to feel warm and close in their relationship in order for them to be in the mood for sex. For these people, sex always has to be lovemaking. If they've been irritated with their spouse or have had an argument, they can't imagine wanting to get close physically. "One argument and she doesn't want to have sex for a week," complains Benjamin. "It's as if she's punishing me!"

"No I'm not," blurts out Lucille. "I'm really not in the mood, and there's nothing I can do about it. I just don't feel very affectionate toward him when we've had a big fight. I guess it takes me time to forget about it, and until then I don't really want to get close."

Although this attitude is understandable and in some sense reasonable, it *is* limiting. As one person said in frustration, "It's like the stars have to be lined up just right in order to have sex."

Lucille was being honest when she said that she wasn't trying to punish Benjamin by not having sex. But when we talked about it further, she realized that she did think of sex as something she *gave* to her partner. If she was still annoyed at Benjamin, she didn't feel like being giving. "I guess it would be different if I thought of sex as something I was *getting* rather than giving. I don't know why, but I don't really think of it that way, even though I do enjoy it. If I thought of it as something that I was doing for myself rather than something I was giving him, I guess I'd have sex a lot more."

The attitude Lucille described is one that many women subscribe to without really thinking about it. If on reflection you realize that you, like Lucille, don't think about sexual pleasure as something for yourself, see what happens if while you are having sex you consciously say to yourself, "This is for me." Sex can be about lovemaking, or it can be simply about physical pleasure. If you think about sex and lovemaking as two *related but different* activities, you will find yourself able to enjoy sex even if you don't feel as close to your spouse as you would like. Even if you're annoyed with your partner, there is no reason to deprive yourself of sexual pleasure.

Chapter 5

We Love Each Other, But . . .
I Have a Hard Time Dealing with My Partner's Emotional Hang-ups

Many people feel that the main problem in their relationship is their spouse's emotional hang-ups. Perhaps you think your difficulties stem from your partner's insecurities, moodiness, anxiety, temper, self-doubts, perfectionism, compulsiveness, or excessive dependency. Though one of you may have more unresolved emotional problems than the other, everybody enters into intimate relationships carrying *some* emotional baggage.

Very frequently couples start to have problems because they each, without knowing it, do things that tap into the other's particular sensitivities. We each bring to intimate relationships expectations and reactions that relate to our upbringings. Our feelings, hopes, and expectations have their roots in earlier relationships with our parents and siblings. Often, the inadvertent clash of emotional issues explains the intense difficulties that a couple may have. The sensitivities people bring to relationships can act like land mines—if we step on one accidentally we are hit with a sudden explosion. This chapter will show you how to locate the land mines in your relationship, walk around them, and defuse them whenever possible.

Let's take a look at four couples and learn how their emotional histories interact in problematic ways.

Four Stories

Mark and Tina

Mark and Tina have been married for three years. It's Mark's second marriage—he is forty-three and has a nine-year-old daughter. Tina, who is twenty-seven, frequently feels that Mark isn't paying any attention to her. "I think he's glad I'm there, though I'm not always sure of it. When I tell him that I'm hurt by how he ignores me, he says that I'm crazy, and we get into a big fight. But I know I'm not." As we talk about this further, it becomes clear that when she and Mark are *alone* she doesn't feel ignored or insignificant. The feelings occur when they are socializing with friends (mostly his friends) and when they have his daughter, Steffie, with them for the weekend. "I know I can seem jealous," Tina says, "but I don't think it's really jealousy. I *know* Steffie needs attention, and she's a great kid. It's that Mark completely ignores me when other people are around—I don't exist for him. Honestly, he wouldn't know if I disappeared. In fact, sometimes I do go off somewhere and it's a long time before he comes looking for me. Then he has the nerve to be furious with *me* for disappearing."

"Tina is incredibly insecure," says Mark. "Unless she has my complete attention she thinks she's not important to me. I know it has to do with the fact that her mother and father both neglected her and sent her to live with relatives on and off for her whole life. But I can't make up for that," he says. "I know I'm much older than she is, but I really thought I was marrying an adult. I don't want to have to be her father or mother. I can be sympathetic up to a point. I know she still feels awkward with my friends because they are friends I've had for twenty years, and a lot of them are still friends with my first wife."

"I try to understand, but I lose it when she launches into how insensitive I am, how I don't know how to be nurturant, how I'm self-centered and oblivious to what she needs. Those types of accusations really get to me. She pushes my buttons. And frankly, when she goes off to pout I don't feel sorry for her at all. It just makes me more mad."

Tina knows that she often feels insignificant and fears abandonment. Her parents lived together for only the first year of her life. After that she was shuttled between each of them and both sets of grandparents. When she was fourteen, her maternal grandparents, with whom she had been living, died in a car accident. By then her mother, who at thirty-three acted more like an older sister, was settled, and Tina moved in with her. Three years later her mother developed cancer and Tina, at seventeen, took charge completely. She had always been a responsible child. "I *had* to be," she said. "My parents were so irresponsible that when I spent time with either of them I always had to watch out for them. I'd worry that my mother would fall asleep with a cigarette in her mouth, or that my father would get into an accident because he'd been drinking. I'd make him wear a seat belt."

So Tina's sensitivity to being ignored was, as Mark had said, completely understandable. Mark tried to be tolerant of Tina's neediness, but had trouble dealing with her reactions when she felt hurt. He had worried about getting involved with such a young woman, but she had seemed so mature. He knew her history and understood that she had grown up fast. "Even though she was only twenty-two when we met, in many ways she seemed more mature than me. She had just lost her mother, whom she'd been taking care of throughout her illness. I couldn't get over how steady and wise she seemed. Maybe I do expect her to be more self-sufficient than she is capable of," said Mark.

When Tina accused Mark of being uncaring, he felt hurt. She had touched on a sensitive spot for him. In fact, she used almost the same words his first wife used when he decided to leave the marriage. She tapped right into his own insecurities and self-doubts. Was he a selfish person? Had he put his own interests before those of his young daughter? And what about the fact that he didn't visit his elderly mother very often? Her Alzheimer's had advanced so much that she no longer recognized him, but he still felt guilty about it. And like so many people, when Mark felt guilty he warded off the feeling by counterattacking.

Dahlia and Fred

Dahlia complained that she couldn't take Fred's sarcasm. "He's completely unpredictable. He can be so warm and nice and then he turns on me like a snarling dog. There's a meanness in his voice and I feel like poison arrows are coming at me. I don't know what he's mad about. Nothing has happened, but he's on the attack. Sarcasm is really hard for me to take. I just hate it. Sometimes I think it would be better if he'd scream at me instead! I'm sure I wouldn't like that either, but I'd prefer it to his icy, sarcastic voice. When he talks that way, I have to leave. I don't want to be around him because he scares me. Actually, I'm revolted by the way he acts. He's not yelling but he's being a bully anyway."

Fred agrees (without apparent embarrassment) that he becomes mean and sarcastic. According to him, however, it's not out of the blue. He says he responds that way because Dahlia nags incessantly, and he tries to ignore it until he just can't take it anymore. "I know she does it because she's anxious. I try to be patient, but when she asks me over and over about things I've already told her I start to get really annoyed. It's like I'm a kid and she's making sure that I do my homework. She talks in a weird tone of voice sometimes, like a schoolteacher. She talks down to me, saying her words slowly and carefully. I don't know exactly how to explain it, but it feels like she thinks she's better than me. I can only stop her with sarcasm."

Nobody likes sarcasm, but it's clear that Dahlia has a particularly strong reaction to it. As we discuss this, she connects the feeling of revulsion to feelings she had as a child when her alcoholic father terrorized the family. She knows that there's a big difference between sarcasm and threats of physical violence, yet they make her feel the same.

Fred, on the other hand, is particularly attuned to being treated in a condescending way. His mother always used to refer to Fred's father as "my third child," and Fred's father would look embarrassed when she said this but never put a stop to it. Watching his mother demean his father made him furious at both of them. "What's *wrong* with her, and why doesn't he put a stop to it? It's not just her words, it's the way she's treated him his whole life.

"Besides that," Fred explained, "I was the poor kid in a rich neighborhood. My father was the superintendent in a fancy building, and although most of the tenants were polite I could see that they looked down on us. I went to the local public school, and the other kids in the building went to private schools. I didn't care. I loved my school. It's just that I felt as if I was second class. For years I had what some people call a chip on my shoulder. If someone treated me as if I wasn't important, I'd rip them apart—not physically, but with words. When Dahlia treats me without respect I have to stop her, and I do it with sarcasm."

Artie and Pat

"Artie explodes over the tiniest things and starts cursing at me," says Pat. "When he's cooled off hours later, he acts like nothing happened and expects me to forget about it, too."

"I know I shouldn't explode, but Pat is so unbelievably insulting sometimes. I bought the wrong type of coffee the other day and you'd think I committed a federal offense. One lousy can of coffee leads to, 'You never get things right. What's the matter with you? Don't you *think*? If I don't tell you exactly what to do, you screw it up!' It's insulting and abusive, and I'm not going to take it!"

Pat recognized that her reaction seemed out of proportion to the event. As we talked it became clear that Pat often felt overburdened by responsibilities. "Don't I ever get a chance to be taken care of? Can't someone look after me once in a while?"

The oldest of seven children, Pat had always been good at organizing everyone and making sure that things got done. Everybody in the family leaned on her, including her now-elderly parents. According to Pat, one of the things that attracted her to Artie was that "unlike the other men I'd gone out with, he was clearly *really* competent." He had risen to regional manager of a chain of retail stores and, like Pat, seemed to know how to get things done. She thought she had married someone who wouldn't be overly dependent on her and whom she could lean on a bit.

As so often happens, however, once children enter the picture men and women start assuming their traditional roles. Pat, who had decided to stay at home for a year after their baby was born, now pretty much handled everything regarding the home and family. It's not that she minded—she felt lucky to be able to stay home and appreciated the fact that Artie's success at his job made that possible. But she did feel that Artie had become dependent on her for instructions when it came to anything about the baby or the house. "Where do you keep the sugar?" he would call from the kitchen. And though it seemed like no big deal to answer, it really irked her. "Where do *you* keep the sugar?" she thought. "What are you, a *guest* here?" And when he took care of the baby for a few hours on the weekend she had to write out exactly what to feed him and when to put him down for a nap. She knew, of course, that Artie was a competent, reliable, really good guy but somehow he was acting more and more like her family. "Ask Pat. She knows." That was the refrain she grew up with and now it was happening again with her husband.

So Pat's outburst about the coffee was just the tip of the iceberg. She felt upset that once again she was "in charge," and though she knew that Artie was a supportive, reliable person, she no longer felt that he ever took care of her.

Artie's reaction to Pat's outburst was also, he agreed, "somewhat" extreme. Despite Artie's accomplishments at his job, he was sensitive to charges of incompetence. He often felt that his success was more a matter of his having been in the right place at the right time rather than his being especially skillful. Growing up in a home with two demanding and highly critical parents, Artie was susceptible to feelings of inadequacy. His father was a perfectionist and nothing Artie did was ever quite right in his father's eyes. Whether it was how Artie mowed the lawn, hammered a nail, or studied in school, it was never good enough. But his parents were also loving and warm and had tried their best, so how could he be mad at them? They were no more critical of him than they were of themselves, so what right did he have to complain? The occasional time when he did have an outburst, his parents were hurt and shocked. They handled it by acting as if nothing happened. Conflict and anger were not allowed in his family.

Artie's behavior after an angry outburst clashed directly with how Pat was brought up. When she and her siblings fought—a frequent occurrence—they talked about it until one person actually apologized. She found it disturbing that Artie could scream at her and then act as if nothing had happened.

Roberta and Martin

Roberta was a lawyer specializing in litigation. She was known in her law firm as tough and unflappable. Every so often, however, Roberta had a little emotional collapse. She never let it happen at the office, but sometimes at home she would have a breakdown. She would cry, yell, and throw things out of frustration. She would sob and scream, "I'm tired!" When she was in one of these high-strung phases, as she called them, she might explode over something annoying that her boyfriend, Martin, had said and storm out of a restaurant or throw something at him on the street.

Most of the time Roberta and Martin, who had been living together for the past two years, did very well together. But he fluctuated between thinking he wanted to spend the rest of his life with her and feeling that he should end the relationship. Roberta tried not to worry too much about the future, but she felt her biological clock ticking and wanted to be in a relationship that was going somewhere. She felt that part of the stress that led to her outbursts stemmed from her anxiety about whether she and Martin really had a future together. She knew that she wanted to be with Martin, but was disturbed by how coldly he treated her when she was upset. "He's great as long as I'm in a good mood," she said. "But if I'm anxious, depressed, or irritable, I feel like he's not sympathetic at all. In fact I get the feeling that he doesn't like me when I'm not in a perfectly fine mood. He seems judgmental and critical at those times and as far from loving as a person can be. I really love him, but the fact that he's so uncaring at those times hurts me a lot. I guess I can live with it, but if he'd be a little comforting instead of critical, I think I'd get over these upsets a lot faster."

Martin knew he was judgmental and critical when Roberta was under stress. Sometimes he felt bad about his reaction, and other times he felt that his criticism was justified. "She's too self-indulgent about her emotions," said Martin. "I don't respect people who can't control themselves, especially in public. One part of me thinks that she's going through a hard time and I shouldn't take it personally when she lashes out at me. But the other part of me feels she's behaving very immaturely, and I don't like it. I'm not happy being her scapegoat! If her job is too much for her she should quit, not take it out on me!"

Roberta's and Martin's assumptions and expectations about emotional upset were very different. Roberta had a close relationship with her parents but sometimes lashed out at them when she was feeling very stressed. Her parents never got upset about it and learned not to take it seriously. They accepted her behavior and offered some soothing reassurances that actually helped quite a bit. She always snapped out of it within a short while.

Even though Martin knew that Roberta's bad moods would pass, he found them highly disturbing. He worried that these outbursts were a sign of serious mental instability, and that was a big part of his reluctance to make a commitment. He dreaded the idea that he might marry someone who would turn out to have serious emotional problems. When he was eight years old his mother spent several months in a psychiatric hospital, and only after she had shock treatment did she recover from her severe depression. She had been more or less all right ever since, but still didn't handle stress well. She had been on and off medication for depression and anxiety for years, and when Martin's father needed heart surgery, the whole family, including his father, worried about how his mother would deal with it.

Martin would tell himself that Roberta was really nothing like his mother, but nevertheless he worried that these emotional phases were a warning of worse things to come. When Roberta had a "meltdown," Martin felt a physical sense of dread. He became anxious and overwhelmed and was in no position to reassure her because he needed reassurance himself. And he was angry not only because he thought she was being self-indulgent but also because she was making him extremely anxious about the future.

Knowing Your Partner's Hot Spots

The first step in avoiding these tangles is to know your partner's specific sensitivities. Think carefully about what has led to trouble in the past. What are the things that your partner seems particularly reactive to? Be sure to include in your list as much detail as possible. For instance, perhaps you feel that your partner doesn't respond well to you when you're feeling down. Try to think about whether this is universally true or whether it depends on the situation. Perhaps your spouse reacts badly when you feel down about something that has to do with the children, but not when you are upset about your job.

Be sure to include in your list even things that you may think are trivial but that seem to bother your partner. Take a few weeks to prepare it since things will occur to you as they happen.

Remember, put down anything that seems to set your partner off even if you think she is being oversensitive or silly. Often particular words have emotional resonances that trigger negative reactions. Try to notice which words and phrases your partner reacts to badly.

To help you prepare your list of your partner's "hot spots," I have included here a list of some of the more common sensitivities that I have encountered in working with couples. I have provided this list to help stimulate you to think about your partner's sensitivities. But you will find additional things to put on your list that are not included in this one.

Common Hot Spots That Lead to Arguments

- Your partner feels that you ignore him in social situations.
- Your partner interprets clutter and mess in the house to mean that you do not care about what is important to her.
- Your partner is a stickler for accuracy. When you exaggerate to make your point, he gets angry and dismissive.
- When you have what seems to you like a mild argument with your child, your spouse gets very upset. She can't stand bickering.
- Your partner gets annoyed if you ask what he is thinking or feeling.
- Your partner gets angry if you say, "I don't want to talk about it," and walk out of the room.
- Your partner can't stand what she calls "endless" discussion about problems.
- Your partner responds very negatively if, to make your point, you tell him what other people have said or thought (e.g., "Even your best friend thinks you are sarcastic").

- Your partner never lets a cutting tone or sarcasm roll off her back.
- Your partner becomes very sensitive when you say that he is performing some task incorrectly.
- Your partner can feel overburdened by responsibility.
- Your partner responds negatively to "hysterical" emotions.
- If you tell your partner that he is being selfish, self-centered, abusive, uncaring, not nice, you get a bad reaction, not the apology you were expecting.
- Your partner reacts badly if you say she seems depressed, anxious, or worried.

Understanding Your Own Contribution to the Problem

Of course it's always easier for us to see our partner's role in relationship problems than it is to see what we contribute to the difficulties. Even when the people I work with have been in individual therapy, they are always taken aback by the question I put to them in the very first meeting: *What do you know about yourself that might contribute to the conflicts that you and your partner have?* Most people know a lot about their own personality, hang-ups, and idiosyncrasies even if they have never studied psychology or been to see a therapist. But people rarely link what they know about themselves to the problematic interactions they have with their spouse. The second step to unravel conflict based on each person's emotional baggage is to work hard at "knowing thyself." For instance:

- Do you tend to feel that you are not the number-one priority in your partner's life?
- Do you feel hurt easily?

- Do you like things done "just so"? Is it hard for you to see things being done the "wrong" way? Is it hard for you to delegate responsibility to someone else?
- Are you afraid of too much closeness or dependency?
- Do you fear abandonment?
- Do you get jealous easily?
- Can you easily feel neglected?
- Do you tend to feel slighted?
- Do you tend to feel that you are being taken advantage of?
- Are you more critical than you would like to be?
- Do you get impatient easily? Do you speak with an edge in your voice when you think your partner should already know something he is asking you?
- Do you see the glass as half-empty rather than half-full?
- Do you have difficulty relaxing until everything on your day's "to do" list is accomplished? Are you a bit compulsive?
- Are you overly sensitive to criticism?
- Do you worry about being "controlled"?
- Do you take on too much responsibility? Do you have difficulty saying no, so that you get overextended?
- Do you push yourself to the point of getting overwhelmed? Do you get tense or even "hysterical" when you feel overextended?
- Do you become very anxious about decisions? Are you obsessive? Do you revisit decisions that have already been made, over and over again?
- Do you mull over what is bothering you for a long time before expressing your feelings?
- Do you blame or lash out when you are frustrated?
- Are you stubborn?
- Are you moody?

- Do you have trouble admitting that you are wrong?
- Is it hard for you to apologize?

All the topics listed under your partner's "hot spots" may apply to you, too.

Five Tips for Using Knowledge of Your Own and Your Partner's Sensitivities to Avoid Arguments

Once you understand your own and your partner's sensitivities, you can use that knowledge to communicate in a way that leads to closeness rather than arguments. These five communication tips will show you how to use your awareness of the emotional baggage you each carry to avoid unnecessary arguments. In addition, if you follow these suggestions each of you will feel better understood and supported by the other.

Tip #1: Even If Your Partner's Sensitivities Seem Irrational, Try to Accommodate Them

When I first say this to the couples I work with, they are a bit alarmed. "I can't and don't want to make up for Tina's childhood," said Mark. "I understand that she had a rough time and felt abandoned. But I'm not her mother or father, and she has to stop distrusting me!" Interestingly enough, Tina agreed. "I don't want to be a ball and chain around Mark's leg. He can't make up for my childhood. But I think he really does tend to ignore me when we are with other people." Of course, Tina and Mark are both right. Mark can't undo Tina's childhood losses. But he might be able to alleviate some of her anxieties, even though they are based much more on past experiences than the current reality.

Here's what I told Tina and Mark: "In my experience, these childhood-based anxieties aren't easy to change. Individual therapy can help, but that can take a long time and is often only partially successful. Tina, you need to recognize your tendency to feel abandoned and try to get a handle on this issue. But while Tina works on this, there *are* things you, Mark, can do to help Tina feel more secure. It's important that we come up with things you can do that will feel okay to you and not like you are being controlled by Tina's problems."

I then asked Tina to tell Mark what little things he could do to help her feel more secure. When Tina first said, "He should pay more attention to me," I explained to her that her suggestion was too general. After some discussion, Tina said that she thought it would help if, when they were socializing, Mark touched her from time to time on her arm or shoulder to let her know that even when he was engrossed in a conversation with someone else *he had not forgotten about her.* Tina and Mark came up with a private signal that Tina could use (she'd squeeze his hand) when she was feeling as if she didn't exist, and he would then make more of an effort to bring her into the conversation.

If, for instance, your partner tends to feel that her needs are being disregarded when the house becomes messy, you should not tell your partner she is being compulsive. Instead, try your best to accommodate this sensitivity and let your partner know that you take her concerns seriously. You might tell your partner that you are straightening up before she arrives home. Or you might ask if there are one or two areas in the house that are particularly important to her and try hard to keep those areas neater.

Or, for instance, if your partner tends to be overly concerned with pleasing others and then feels overwhelmed and resentful because she has said yes to more than she can handle, you might try to help by asking her to think about your requests before saying yes. You can remind your partner that you won't feel upset if she says no.

The main point is that if you think about where you can comfortably and creatively accommodate to your partner's emotional issues, the snowballing effect that they have produced in the past does not have to happen. This does not mean that either of you needs to or should do all the accommodating. Each of you also has the responsibility to work on your own issues, otherwise accommodations will turn into submission and that in itself will create further tension. So in order for accommodations to work, your partner must feel that you are working hard on your own issues and that the task of solving your problems has not been passed along to him.

Tip #2: Prevent Automatic Emotional Reactions by Taking into Account What You Know About Your Partner

In the case of Pat and Artie, we saw that Artie was particularly vulnerable to feeling incompetent and that when Pat expressed her frustrations about his lack of initiative around household responsibilities he heard her criticisms as confirmation of his incompetence. If instead Pat prefaced her comments with a statement that reminded Artie of what she admired, he would react less to her criticism. She could say, for instance, "I know you are terrific about handling our finances and many other things, but it really upsets me that you don't know what to do when I leave you alone with the baby." Or perhaps she might say, "I know you do your job really well—I've heard your employees talk about how smart you are—but at home I feel like you don't think about what needs to be done." Criticism is always hard to take, but it is particularly difficult if it taps into self-doubts and anxieties that go beyond the specifics of the complaint. The preface helps interrupt the tendency to overgeneralize.

So, if you know that your partner hates thinking of himself as someone who cannot control his emotions, you might say, "I know you try hard to be even-tempered and most of the time I think you do pretty well, but recently I've been feeling that you've been moody and sullen with me." If your partner is sensitive to being told that he is too selfish or self-centered, you can preface your statement with something like, "I know that you think about my needs a lot and that it's important to you to not be self-centered, but I felt that what you did yesterday ignored my needs." Or simply, "I know you are a really good person, but what you did yesterday wasn't nice."

Tip #3: Acknowledge Your Own Sensitivities and Turn Criticisms into Requests

Often you can avoid highly charged conflict by prefacing your reactions, comments, and criticism with a statement that acknowledges your own sensitivities. Tina knew that she was prone to feeling insignificant. Even if she felt that Mark really was ignoring her, a preface that acknowledges her particular sensitivities and needs would help Mark be more receptive to her criticism. Tina could say something like, "I know I need more attention in those situations than a lot of people do" or "I know I easily feel abandoned, and I really felt you weren't paying enough attention to me given how much I need it."

Roberta knew that she had small breakdowns from time to time and that she always recovered. If, even in the middle of a meltdown, Roberta told Martin that she was just in a high-strung phase and would be okay after a while, she would quell some of Martin's anxiety, and he would be able to respond in a more caring manner.

In general, the more you can couch your request as having to do with *your needs* rather than your partner's failings, the more likely you are to be heard. If you say, for instance, "I know I get stressed by a messy environment and am a bit compulsive," your partner will probably try harder to keep things neat than if you accuse him of being inconsiderate or a slob.

If you know that you have a sensitivity about being controlled, it would help to say something like, "You know I have a thing about being told what to do, so even though what you're doing probably wouldn't bother someone else it annoys me. I'd appreciate it if you wouldn't give me directions and advice when I'm driving."

Tip #4: Avoid "Fighting Words"

Do you remember in the old Westerns when a gunfight was preceded by one cowboy saying to the other, "Those are fightin' words, pardner"? Most of us know what words and accusations will set off a fighting stance in our partner. Even if you think your partner often overreacts and shouldn't be so sensitive, *don't say things that almost always lead to trouble.* This may seem obvious, but in my work with couples I have seen that people often keep doing and saying exactly what has always received a bad reaction.

Dahlia knows that Fred is sensitive to being talked to in a condescending tone. She should therefore make a promise to herself that no matter how frustrated she feels, she will not use a "teacherlike" tone.

Martin reacts badly to what he calls hysteria. It's important, then, for Roberta to try not to express her upset in highly emotional language or exaggerated statements.

If your partner responds negatively whenever you say something like "You look depressed, what's the matter?" then you
should make sure you ask about his feelings in a way that won't
touch off his defensiveness. The word *depressed* might have
connotations that set him off, so perhaps he would respond better
if you said, "You look a little down, is anything the matter?" If
your partner responds badly to being told that he is unapprecia-
tive, perhaps because he thinks you sound like his long-suffering
mother, then simply eliminate that word from your vocabulary
when trying to convey your feelings to him. Or if telling your
partner he is being *uncaring, compulsive, inconsiderate,* or *selfish*
only leads to countercriticisms, then vow to yourself that you will
not use those phrases in the future.

I have found that using the word *abusive* often gets a bad
reaction. Before accusing your partner of being verbally abusive,
ask yourself if the words insulting, hurtful, or cruel would work
just as well. The word *abusive* has become somewhat overused
and may say to your partner that you think he is a monster.
Unless you think this is true it is better to describe his actions in
some other way.

Tip #5: Don't Make Psychological Interpretations of Your Partner's Behavior

Most people do not welcome (to put it mildly) psychological
interpretations of their behavior. Even if you have a correct take
on your partner's behavior, don't volunteer your understanding
of what is happening. Not many of us like to think that we don't
know our own feelings. The most challenging part of being a
therapist is finding the right way to make interpretations so that
they will be considered seriously and not experienced as an
attack. When one's own partner makes interpretations, they will

probably be dismissed—or worse, seen as criticism. This makes sense because you, as the spouse, are not coming from a neutral place. So if you say to your partner, "I think what you did was passive-aggressive," he will see it as your reading something hostile into behavior that he believes was not intended to be aggressive. He may feel hurt or outraged that you misunderstand his intentions. Even if you are right you won't get anywhere with this kind of discussion.

Similarly, if you tell your partner that he is reacting to you as if you were his controlling mother, he will feel that you are blind to your own behavior and that his irritation has nothing to do with his mother! The title of this book was originally going to be *Never Say She's Just Like Her Mother*, since this type of accusation represents the type of thing couples say that adds fuel to the fire. Seeing connections between your partner's behaviors and that of his parents, even if not said in anger, is not the type of understanding that most of us look for from our mates!

How to Be in Control of Your Feelings

"I can't help what I feel, I just feel it!" is a comment that I hear over and over again from the couples I work with. Tina felt she could learn not to tell Mark that she felt unimportant, "but that won't make the feeling go away." And Dahlia couldn't imagine not responding in her gut to Fred's sarcasm. Similarly Artie said that although he would try to control his temper when he thought Pat was talking down to him, he didn't see how he could feel anything but anger in that circumstance. Most people, like Tina, Artie, and Dahlia, regard their feelings as something inherent and beyond their control. Something happens and the feeling occurs, unbeckoned and often unwanted. Although they have a choice about whether or not to act on or express the feeling, many people don't think they have a choice about whether or not to *have* the feeling.

We all know that feelings can change rapidly in response to new information. If you are angrily brooding because your friend is late for lunch, the anger will readily give way to concern when you start to think that he is never late and something must have happened to him. What we think directly affects our feelings— the school of cognitive psychotherapy was founded on this principle. If, for instance, we believe that the shove we received while looking for a seat in a movie theater was accidental, we do not feel the same as we would if we thought the person was trying to push ahead to get a better seat. If your spouse's inattentiveness comes across as a sign that he is bored with you, you will feel hurt. If you think instead that he is preoccupied with work, you will have a different feeling. You may still feel neglected, but you won't be nearly as hurt.

I tell the couples who consult me that feelings can be modified and I can help them learn how, but first they have to decide whether they actually *want* to change the feeling. Would you rather feel less hurt, less angry, or less disappointed in your spouse?

This is not as easy to answer as you might initially think. Many people believe that what they feel is the truth, and if they alter their feelings they put on blinders. Others do not want to decrease the intensity of what they feel, because if they are too easygoing their partner will not be motivated to work on the relationship. And some people can't believe that their feelings could change; they think they would only be playacting.

You should consider my offer to help you change your feelings for the following reasons. First of all, negative feelings are unpleasant. Most people prefer to feel up instead of down, relaxed rather than tense, and calm rather than angry. Second, negative feelings make other people feel bad, too. Everyone in the family affects everyone else's mood in one way or another. Most important, although it is possible that your anger, hurt, and upset will be responded to positively by your spouse and motivate him to act differently in the future, negative feelings more *often* have negative effects rather than positive ones. When Tina expressed intense hurt that Mark ignored her, he became angry, not supportive. And Roberta's minibreakdowns scared Martin and made him feel more distant.

People often have a valid concern about playacting. But if you try the "feeling-change" strategies described below, you will not be playacting at all. The following methods will help you to change your feelings about something.

Stop building your case. This state of mind focuses on those things that confirm *your* point of view. You look for more and more evidence to justify how you feel. For instance, if you feel neglected because your partner has worked late for several nights you might start to focus on all of the other ways he has neglected you. You then prepare a speech in your head in which you accuse, try, and convict your spouse of neglect. And strangely, this often feels gratifying. You may feel pleasure, or something akin to pleasure, in proving that you have been wronged.

So, the first step in changing your feelings requires you to stop proving your point to yourself or to him. Remind yourself that you have little to gain in painting a portrait in which your partner is a bad guy. You might make him feel bad, but you will feel equally bad. Do you really want to crush the good feelings you have for your partner with the weight of your arguments? The problem with making a case against your spouse is that if you win, you also lose, because you have worked yourself up into an unhappy state of mind.

Try to notice the kernels of alternative feelings you also have. Even when you feel very upset, you will probably find that you have fleeting thoughts and feelings that are quite different from the negative ones currently dominating your psyche. When Tina feels that Mark doesn't care about her, she probably *also* has the passing thought that it isn't really true. She thinks for a moment that he's ignoring her because he feels guilty about not seeing his child enough. Or she has a moment of thinking, "Oh, forget it, of course he loves me." Try to notice if you have some feelings that contradict the more dominant negative ones, and don't push them away in order to build your case.

Argue with yourself. Use your mind to combat what you feel. Most people welcome alternate explanations that allow them to feel less upset. Think about a conversation you would have with a friend when you're angry at your spouse. Your friend might say, "Maybe he's worried about his job and that's why he's so withdrawn." Or you tell your friend that you're so angry at your husband that you're thinking of separating, but she reminds you that most of the time your husband is really considerate and caring. Maybe you tell your friend that you're not in love with your partner and she tells you that she read somewhere that everybody feels that way sometimes, and you shouldn't assume that the loving feelings won't return. A good friend can help you gain perspective on the situation rather than merely echo what you already feel.

If you consciously think about talking to yourself the way a good friend would to help you gain perspective, you will find that it is easier than you might have thought to feel better about something that is upsetting you.

Make an effort to put yourself in a better mood. I routinely ask the people who consult me, "What works for you? What can help put you in a better mood?" Often these questions surprise them. Many people are not accustomed to making a conscious effort to change their mood. Yet, with just a little prompting, most people find that they do have ideas about what works for them. The main point here is that consciously making an effort to better your mood is not running away from your problems. After you've exercised, for instance, seen a movie, or listened to some lively music, you are likely to have a somewhat different feeling about what has upset you, and you will be able to approach the problem with a positive state of mind.

Treating Your Partner's Vulnerabilities as Opportunities to Be Loving

Thus far we have covered emotional baggage and conflicts based on avoiding one another's hot spots. But couples can also use a knowledge of each other's emotional sensitivities to greatly strengthen the bond of love. Often small actions can have deep emotional significance, and with some thought, emotionally sensitive gestures can have a big impact. For example, if your partner tends to be a caretaker who gets overwhelmed by all her responsibilities, she will welcome gestures that say, in effect, "I am looking after you." One woman who managed a division of a large corporation shyly confessed that she loved it when her husband wrapped a scarf around her neck before she ventured out into the cold. Another person told me that the one-minute-long "How are you doing?" phone calls from his wife while he was at work meant a tremendous amount to him. My own husband lays out my vitamins for me every night, and though I know this has become a ritual it never fails to make me feel cared for.

Think about what warms your partner's heart. Does your partner tend to push himself too hard? Does he need a pat on the back for his hard work, or some encouragement to slow down? Does she feel good when you worry that she isn't getting enough sleep? Does your partner need encouragement to take time off for herself? Does your partner have trouble buying things for or making time for himself without feeling selfish? Suggesting that he do something for himself will be a true emotional gift.

Each time you offer support rather than criticism when your partner has made a mistake, you deepen intimacy and love. If your partner is searching for her keys and is upset with herself for being disorganized, it will help immensely if you simply help her look for them rather than focus in on her self-blame. Some friends of mine told me that when one of them drops and breaks something the other will clean it up, since the one who dropped it "feels bad enough."

Often I hear men say that they would like to nurture their wife, but they don't really know what they need to do. One man who grew up with a loving and nurturant mother understood when I asked him if he could act with his wife the way his mother acted with him. In short I am suggesting that you treat your partner's vulnerabilities as opportunities to be loving.

Chapter 6

We Used to Love Each Other, But . . .
Now I'm Not So Sure

There are few experiences as painful as living day in and day out in a relationship that makes you unhappy. Many of the people who come to see me are terribly distressed by how chronically disappointed they are in their marriages. It is extremely painful to be married to someone you feel you may no longer love or respect and who does not give you what you need. If you are in this type of relationship you may alternate between feelings of rage or even hatred and feelings of despair, futility, depression, and guilt. I have written this chapter for those of you who feel that you have tried to improve your relationship but nothing seems to work.

Sometimes people in relationships of this sort also feel shame. Shame, because they have been spinning their wheels for years, unable to go forward, yet unable to call it quits. Shame about the pettiness of their arguments and the constant tit for tat in which they engage. Shame about the loss of control or venom in their fights. Shame that their children have had to witness emotional, and sometimes physical, abuse. Or even shame that they have lived for years as "friends" and have each accepted a marriage of convenience, without love, sex, or passion.

Many of the people I see feel emotionally tortured by their uncertainty about whether to leave their marriage. Living for years with such tension and hostility can feel like a life sentence. Yet thoughts of separation and divorce fill most people with dread. Worry about the effect on the children, the rage of your spouse, the financial deprivation that so often follows, the cost and stress of litigation, and the nightmare of custody battles can overwhelm the hardiest of souls. Women who want children worry about their meeting someone else in time to start a family. Even if children are not an issue, anxiety about the possibility of spending the rest of your life alone can factor in to the decision to stick it out. Many people have become discouraged about the possibility of any good relationship, and they feel that unless they are prepared to live alone they might as well stay put.

And if you are more unhappy than your partner, you might be concerned he will be devastated if you decide you want to separate. Knowing that he still loves and needs you makes you feel terrible. Except for those times when you are enraged at your partner during an argument, you hate the thought of inflicting hurt and pain on him. The thought of how crushed he will be makes you feel terribly guilty. How will you ever get him to understand why you feel the problems can't be worked out?

If you have had these thoughts, you know that your resolve to try to stay together doesn't last for long. A weekend of fighting, silence, loneliness, or alienation starts you thinking all over again that maybe you should bite the bullet and separate. Maybe you have even contacted a lawyer to discuss your options. Yet you just can't seem to go through with it. And it's not just anxiety about the consequences of such a big decision that deters you. Apologies, a good talk, a pleasant vacation together, or even a few days of warmth give you hope that perhaps things could work out. And at times you have a sense that you still care for your partner and love him deeply. Perhaps divorce, with all its pitfalls, won't be necessary after all.

After working with hundreds and hundreds of couples who have ridden this dizzying and disorienting roller coaster, I can tell you that most (though not all) relationships can be repaired and restored. Warmth and love can return much more easily than you think.

Often what prevents couples from stopping the downward spiral are the vicious cycles that develop when people are hurt and angry. But even one person in the couple can break a pattern of vicious cycles. Small changes in how you act with your partner can lead to changes in his behavior even if he doesn't consciously decide to be different. This chapter will tell you how to start the process of change when you and your partner have been spinning your wheels and going nowhere for years.

If you follow the advice in this chapter, you and your spouse will feel much more hopeful about improving your relationship. Once that occurs, you will then be able to use the tips contained in earlier chapters to sustain the progress you have made. No relationship is perfect and I can't promise that these methods will result in an idyllic life together. But I *can* tell you that they will help you enormously in getting out of repetitive and depressing patterns.

Watching Problems Snowball: Three Stories

The first step in getting unstuck is to notice what *you* are doing in response to your partner's actions. Let's take a look at some case examples that may help you identify your own vicious cycles. Watch how each person's reaction to the other's behavior causes the problems to snowball.

Marietta and Max

Marietta, an insurance agent, and Max, a stock trader, had been married for three years. They had gone out with each other a few times many years earlier but both were already involved with someone else. Max married the woman he was dating when he first met Marietta, and that marriage ended in divorce. Marietta also married the person she'd been seeing and she, too, divorced. A couple of years later, Marietta decided to have a baby through artificial insemination. "I was desperate to be a mother, and was worried that if I waited until I met the right person I might never have a child."

Being a single parent had turned out fine, but it made her sad that her son didn't have a father. So when she and Max started seeing each other again after meeting at a party, Marietta couldn't have been happier. She felt extremely comfortable with Max. Even though he was in his late forties, he had a cute, "naughty boy" manner that Marietta found appealing. And he was terrific with two-year-old Sam.

Max was overjoyed to discover that Marietta was now single. He had thought of her often and felt that "the road not taken" was the mistake of his life. Marietta had a reserved, almost mysterious style that Max found intriguing. She was hard to get to know, but her smile and obvious pleasure in his boyishness made him determined to crack her self-contained "I'm fine without anyone" style.

Both of them agreed that when they met again it was like coming home. They felt so comfortable with one another that they decided to marry three months after they started dating. Both felt amazed and grateful for their second chance to be together.

When they appeared in my office three years later, Marietta

had decided almost definitely that she wanted a divorce. Life with Max was unbearable. "He loses his temper over nothing. I know he has an incredibly high-stress job, but I can't take it anymore. He gets frustrated over the most ordinary things and recently he's been screaming at Sam a lot. And he's the most controlling person in the world! *Everything* has to be done exactly the way *he* wants it. I really think he doesn't get it—that *three* people live in this house."

At first Max felt nothing but positive feelings for Sam. He loved the idea of having a son. But soon he began to feel like an outsider. Only Marietta could put Sam to bed, and this entailed actually sleeping in his room for half the night. And Marietta disagreed with the structure and limit-setting that Max felt was necessary to teach a child self-control. Marietta wouldn't back him up when he expected certain things of Sam. She made it clear that Sam was *her* son, not his, and that child-rearing would be done her way.

"I'm incredibly frustrated," said Max. "Marietta is completely unaffectionate. She's built up a wall around her. She's always been reserved, but now it's impossible to break through. She completely ignores what I want. She collects all sorts of things and I can't get her to throw anything out or put it in storage."

"I *am* unaffectionate and closed off to him, that's true," said Marietta. "After we got married he came in and tried to take over. He criticizes everything, from the way I peel carrots to the way I keep my desk—and even the way I talk to my customers on the phone! I was doing fine without him, and then he comes into my house and tries to 'improve' everything. And the boyishness that I found so cute isn't so cute anymore. Basically, he has tantrums if he doesn't get his way. He acts just like my five-year-old. I'm not going to let someone control me, so I ignore him."

Max, who is extremely well-organized and almost compulsively neat, recognizes that he likes things done a certain way. "I guess I am controlling," he says. "But if it's important to me to use a certain pot for making spaghetti, or not to fill the teakettle enough for ten cups when we only need boiled water for two, why can't she do it? She's the most stubborn person in the world. I feel like I just don't count and I guess that makes me even more pushy about having things done my way."

"Most of the time I just don't think about it," says Marietta. "I forget. It's not on purpose, but I guess because I'm so fed up with the constant comments I tune him out."

So the more controlling Max becomes, the less Marietta listens and the more she withdraws affection. With so little affection between them, Max's resentment of the mother-son relationship increases. He becomes more negative about Sam, which only leads Marietta to withdraw more.

Marietta, feeling protective of her son, is less strict with him than she might otherwise be, which results in Max becoming more of the disciplinarian in the family. Although clearly Max must assume responsibility for his own loss of temper and compulsiveness, these traits are made worse by the chronic feeling that Marietta ignores him. And Marietta's overinvolvement with Sam is made worse by her sense of alienation from Max.

Linda and Kevin

Linda and Kevin had been married for five years. They met when Linda temped in Kevin's consulting firm. "He was so smart," said Linda. "I mean really smart. And not just because he has an MBA—he knows about everything. I always had trouble with school. When I concentrated I'd do okay, but honestly, I liked to party. Somehow I managed to graduate, but it was never easy for me. When I met Kevin I was excited by the idea of learning from him and he got a kick out of playing teacher," said Linda.

"I really fell for her," said Kevin. "I'd never met anyone as playful and vivacious as Linda. Or as warm. Or as beautiful. I also enjoyed the way we could hang out without doing much. It was a nice change of pace from my competitive, fast-track career. She helped me to slow down and relax."

As we talked I began to understand what had happened. Kevin, who was assertive at work, tended to be passive when it came to his personal life. "I guess I'm like a lot of men," he said. "I don't keep in touch with friends and I relied on Linda to make plans with people."

Content to blend in with Linda's lifestyle, they spent weekends going to flea markets, shopping, watching TV, and hanging out with Linda's friends. "I guess you could say we spend a lot of time on weekends being couch potatoes. I work long hours during the week and often at the end of the weekend I feel like I didn't do much with the little free time I have."

"I'm willing to do other things but he never plans anything," says Linda. "Instead he complains and puts down my friends for being boring. I admit that he's polite and nice to them but privately he always makes digs about how all we ever talk about is gossip. It's really insulting—and it's not true."

Several vicious cycles had occurred. Kevin's tendency to be passive in relationships lead him ultimately to grow bored with the way they spent their weekends. But instead of dealing with it directly, he became critical and scornful of Linda's friends. This made Linda feel hurt and she was resistant when Kevin suggested that they see her old friends less often. It felt like he was asking her to choose between them and him.

After about a year together Kevin began to spend more and more time at the office. He'd have a quick bite to eat and then work until ten o'clock. He didn't mind the long hours and had some good friends in the office from before he got married, and sometimes he had dinner with friends from business school or college.

"I joined them for dinner a few times but all they talked about were mergers and acquisitions, which they find *endlessly* fascinating," said Linda. "And when we went out with his friends from college they talked about topics that I didn't know anything about. I'd feel really dumb, and Kevin never tried to bring me into the conversation or explain what they were talking about. I felt bad about myself after these dinners and realized how different Kevin and I are."

"Linda takes the fact that I work late personally. But I've always worked this way; it's just that our first year together I worked less than I normally did. And as far as meeting my friends for dinner, Linda's insecure for no reason. Everyone likes her."

Kevin, feeling rejected, pulled away from Linda by spending even more time at work. The more time Kevin spent at his office, the more Linda felt that he wasn't really interested in her. She withdrew from him and looked to her family and friends for validation. Feeling insecure, hurt, and rejected, Linda became more determined to be herself. She resisted what she regarded as his efforts to get her to be more cultured.

Kevin wanted to accept Linda for who she was and felt guilty about feeling bored with how they spent their time. His guilt and anger resulted in passive behavior when they were together. He tried to please her by doing what *she* wanted when they were together. He watched TV with her when he preferred to read. He went shopping with her and tried to accommodate to what she wanted. But the more he did this, the worse both of them felt. She sensed his boredom and thought he was being patronizing.

Both Kevin and Linda felt more appreciated for who they were with other people rather than with each other. Linda, who now worked as a party planner for a public relations firm, was doing really well. She had been promoted three times in the last year and a half and started going out with her own friends after work. They made her feel funny and smart.

By the time Linda and Kevin came to me they had both stopped expecting much from one another. They hadn't had any sexual contact in months. When they did spend time together, they wound up bickering. They felt depressed, lonely, and resentful of the wasted years. Each accused the other of wishing to separate but not wanting to be the first to give up on the marriage.

Sandra and June

Sandra and June had been friends ever since they met in college. Sandra, a lesbian who had come out to her family in her teens, had recently broken up with a woman she had been living with for the past three years. June was unhappily married to a verbally abusive and alcoholic man. She had two young sons and felt trapped in a bad marriage. "Sandra helped me take hold of the situation," said June. "We met for dinner every couple of weeks and it was like therapy for me. She helped me find the courage to leave Jimmy and figure out how I was going to make ends meet. During that period something changed between us. We weren't just friends anymore. I fell in love with her, and I realized that I'd been pushing away that feeling for a long time because I felt so scared about being attracted to a woman."

"The first couple of years together were tough," said Sandra. "We had a big custody battle on our hands, and June's ex didn't give one penny toward the support of the boys until we got a court order."

Sandra made significantly more money than June. She was a

lawyer and worked for a prestigious firm, while June worked part-time in an art gallery to have more time with her sons. "I supported everyone, but I really didn't mind," said Sandra. "I loved June and the kids so much. The kids are both really smart and did well in school. But kids are expensive!"

Sandra and June came from very different backgrounds. Sandra's parents, who had adopted four children, were calm, loving, and supportive.

In contrast, June grew up in a home where the main thing communicated was rage. "My parents fought constantly and my father became really mean after a couple of drinks. He never hit my mother, but he did hit us. We never knew when he would explode over something. He punched me a few times but mostly beat my older brother. Both my brothers were in a rage, and they took it out on the girls and each other. It was hell. And my mother was constantly angry and depressed. Nothing but criticism came out of her mouth. I couldn't wait to grow up and get out of there. I escaped in my books and school. I buried my head in my homework or in novels as much as possible and tried to ignore everything else."

Sandra and June came to see me because now they were in a rage at each other. They had been together for over five years and didn't want to split up, but seemed headed in that direction.

"I'm just not getting what I need from June," said Sandra. "I have a high-stress job and even though I've been 'out' right from the beginning, I don't feel completely accepted and comfortable at the very traditional law firm where I work. When I come home I want to relax and unwind. It drives me crazy to find the dishes still in the sink and the house a mess. I don't mind supporting June and the kids but I think it's only fair for her to take care of things at home. But I probably wouldn't mind the mess as much if she was there for me emotionally when I got home. I'd like to be able to talk to her. It's not that the kids take all her attention—they're teenagers now and not even around that much. June just doesn't seem to want to be with me. She's always going to meetings for different organizations at night, and if she's home she's on the phone or reading a book. She doesn't seem to *need* to talk to me much. In some ways I'm much closer to some of my friends than I am to June. I want more from a relationship than this. It's just not enough."

"All I get from Sandra is criticism," said June bitterly. "She's unhappy about how I live my life. She complains that I'm disorganized, do things at the last minute, and waste time on unimportant things. If I don't do it her way, then something's wrong with me."

Sandra felt that frequently June was silently angry and wouldn't acknowledge it. But June thought that Sandra was the angry one. "If I'm home an hour after I said I would be, she goes into a tirade about how selfish, self-centered, and spoiled I am."

"She doesn't seem to understand that people say things when they are mad that they might not really mean," said Sandra in response.

June described always feeling guilty about doing activities that took her away from home. "I'm always worried that Sandra will be mad that I'm taking time away from us."

"I get mad," said Sandra, "because even when she *is* home she's not really there, and I'm always the one who has to shape my plans around her schedule. I feel like I have to fit myself into her life. Our relationship is imbalanced—I give a lot more than I receive."

Both June and Sandra felt discouraged and furious. "I'm tired of Sandra saying that she's thinking about separating." said June.

"If she's not getting enough out of it, then I can't do anything about that. I'll be devastated if we break up, but I'll survive."

"I feel terrible about breaking up. And I still love June, but I'm miserable."

Sandra and June wanted to give their relationship one last shot. They couldn't understand how love had turned into such bitterness. They both felt terribly hurt by the other. Feeling that her emotional needs weren't being met, Sandra became increasingly angry at June for her failure to take care of practical things. The more critical Sandra became, the more June resorted to her way of handling attack—to withdraw and spend time outside the house. And the more she did that, the more critical Sandra became. June, angry in return, would become even more distant and emotionally unavailable.

Four Tips for Getting Change Started

These three couples were stuck. Things kept getting worse and worse. All of them wished they could find a way to make things right again, but were pessimistic about turning things around in their relationship. If you feel that way, here are some tips for how you can start the process of change, even without your partner's help.

Tip #1: Make Changes Even If Your Partner Doesn't

Many couples remain stuck because neither person wants to change until their partner does. Marietta, for instance, said in a session, "I'm not going to be physically affectionate when he acts the way he does. When he stops being so critical, I'll be warmer." But waiting for the other to make changes *first* often gets the couple into a deeper and deeper hole. The vicious cycle needs to be broken somewhere, and getting into a power struggle over who makes the first step toward change is ultimately self-defeating.

For instance, if Linda decided to greet Kevin warmly instead of remaining on the phone when he comes home, she would be breaking a vicious cycle that they have gotten into.

It may take a while for your partner to notice and respond to your gesture of goodwill. Be patient. Don't return to your old way of acting because your partner didn't immediately act differently in return. Often it takes time for your partner to register your changed behavior. Anger and discouragement take time to lift. You must maintain your commitment to change your part in the vicious cycle for at least four to six weeks before concluding that it hasn't made any difference in how your partner treats you.

Tip #2: Remember the Proverb "You Catch More Flies with Honey Than with Vinegar"

Everybody responds better to praise than to criticism. The most common characteristic of stuck relationships is that each person keeps trying to motivate the other through criticism. But if you use praise instead, you will start the process of change.

Of course, when couples have reached the point of chronic anger and discouragement that we saw in the three couples described earlier, they usually don't feel that there is anything to praise. The trick is to notice any step in the right direction, no matter how small it is. There are two parts to this process. First, you must learn to notice the smallest step in the right direction. Then, you need to respond positively to that step without tacking on criticism of what hasn't been done or what remains to be done. For example, if Max emptied the dishwasher one night, Linda would say something like, "Thanks, I appreciate your help." She would *not* add, "But I wish you'd do it more often." If June sat and chatted with Sandra for even a few minutes when Sandra came home before getting up to make phone calls, Sandra would say something like, "Oh, it was nice talking like that, it helped me unwind a little." She would not add, "Why are you always in such a hurry to get away?"

When I first present this idea to couples, they view it as unnatural and contrived. But doing what is natural doesn't always get the best results. The fact is that the more praise people receive the more inclined they will be to change. Many people complain that they don't help out with chores or do the things that their spouse would like because they can never do it "right": "I didn't say it exactly right" or "I didn't buy the right thing." Although we all get frustrated when something is done incorrectly, you will help start the process of change if you temporarily ignore your frustration and instead express appreciation.

"Why should I lower my standards?" said Sandra when I suggested that she do this with June. And Marietta said, "Why should I have to manipulate Max's ego to get him to act the way he *should*? It's ridiculous. I don't see why I should treat him with kid gloves!" The answer is simply that if you continue to express anger and criticism your relationship will continue to go downhill.

When your partner feels that he has succeeded in pleasing you, it will encourage him to do more to please you. And as you see more effort on his part, you will be even more open and responsive to him until small steps in the right direction have changed into giant steps.

Tip #3: Be Emotionally Generous

Stuck couples have stopped being nice to one another. Even if you don't consciously punish your spouse for how he has hurt you, you certainly don't treat him the way you would if he were your friend. An important step in the right direction is to decide to be nice to your partner. For instance, if you know that your partner loves a back rub or feels very cared about when you bring home a little gift from a business trip, give it to him even if he doesn't give in return.

Emotional generosity can take many forms. It can mean giving your partner a break on a chore she hates to do. Imagine Linda's surprise if Kevin said after dinner one night, "I'll clean up, you look tired." Emotional generosity can also mean encouraging your partner to participate in an activity he likes even if it means time away from you. If Linda actually encouraged Kevin to play golf one weekend rather than being angry that he was spending more time away from her, he might feel more appreciated.

You could also suggest doing something that your partner would like even if it isn't *your* preference. If you suggest eating in a restaurant that your spouse loves even though it's not one of your favorites, you might surprise and touch your partner with your generous attitude.

Again, do not expect immediate results. It will take time for your spouse to register your newfound generosity. Both of you have come to expect the other to begrudge and keep accounts. But you will defeat the purpose of this generosity if you adopt the attitude, "Look how nice I've been to you and you haven't even appreciated it or been nice to me." So remember to make a serious effort without keeping score.

Tip #4: Walk in Your Partner's Shoes

Another sign of a stuck relationship is when a couple stops listening to each other's point of view. Instead of seriously considering their partner's perspective, they approach their difficulties with an "I'm right, you're wrong" attitude. Feeling misunderstood, mistreated, and unloved, each person answers accusations with counteraccusations, and a competition takes place for who has been most wronged, mistreated, or hurt.

You can break this pattern by trying to understand your partner's complaints from his perspective. Mentally argue his side instead of your own. What bothers him? What does he want? If you were him could you understand his feelings? I always ask couples in my office to listen to each other for what they can agree with, rather than wait for their turn to defend and counterattack. So Marietta tried to understand Max's feelings about setting more limits for her son, and Max was able to see how his anger affected everyone around him.

When one person gives even a little by saying, "I can understand why you feel that way," the process of getting unstuck has begun. But understanding must be followed by action. If you can understand why your partner feels what he does, it's important to *act* on that understanding. If June can understand why Sandra feels lonely when June's out at meetings in the evening, she also needs to do something to help Sandra feel less lonely. And if Marietta understands how Max feels when she continues to do things her way, she should try harder to do some things the way he would like.

Can a Marriage Survive the Betrayal of an Affair?

Affairs shake the foundation of trust upon which marriages are built, but I firmly believe that relationships can survive and even grow stronger after an affair. I am not suggesting that affairs are a good way to start change—they hurt everyone involved. But like it or not affairs happen, and can at times lead to a stronger relationship than the couple had before the affair. Affairs have meanings and implications that are specific to each couple, but some questions come up time and time again. Here are some of the questions I hear most often after an affair:

Q: He says he still loves me and always did, even while he was seeing his girlfriend. I just can't accept that. If he really loved me, why would he do a thing like that?

A: Your spouse's affair may have little to do with his love for you. He may have had the affair because it gave him an ego boost at a time when his self-esteem was low. Perhaps he felt depressed, or old, or confused about where he was going in his life. Or maybe he felt incredibly stressed by career and family responsibilities. These reasons do not excuse the affair, but they can help you understand that your spouse's behavior doesn't mean that he doesn't really love you.

Q: I feel as if she's a different person than I thought she was. I never thought she could lie and scheme the way she did. How do I deal with this? I thought she was a moral person. I thought she had integrity and was always honest with me. How could I have been so wrong about her? I feel like I don't even know her anymore when I think about how she lied right to my face. How could such a reliable and honest person act this way?

A: Many people of otherwise good character have affairs. The combination of intense emotion and rationalization leads people to act out of character. When the affair started she probably convinced herself that it wouldn't affect your relationship and that you wouldn't find out. But lying and having sex outside the marriage profoundly affects a relationship.

I have seen people who are honest in all other areas of their lives weave a complex web of lies to justify having a relationship outside the marriage. People can be good parents, trustworthy business partners, loyal friends, and generous, caring individuals and still have affairs.

Your spouse is still the same person in all other respects. But is this like saying, "She's a wonderful person except for the fact that she killed someone"? I don't know the answer to that. Perhaps you will say, "I can forgive her, but I'll never think of her with as much respect again." This depends on your own moral and religious code.

Q: In a way, the lies and stories he told me are the worst part. I feel humiliated by being lied to like that. He made a fool of me. I'm furious and don't know if I can ever get over being played with that way. Even if he had told me the truth when I asked directly, it would have been better. Do people ever get over this horrible feeling of being manipulated?

A: Yes, but it takes time. You may be so angry and hurt that it is initially impossible for you to accept your partner's explanation for why he deceived and manipulated you. People give themselves many reasons for being dishonest to their partner. Some of the most common reasons for lying are: "The affair makes me happier, and thus easier to live with," "This has nothing to do with my marriage or my love for my spouse," "She doesn't really want to know—that's why she doesn't ask me any questions about where I'm going or what I'm doing," "I'm going to end it soon, so why should I cause my spouse pain?" If you have heard these types of explanations, you probably thought they were nothing more than excuses and self-serving rationalizations. Understandably, you may feel that your partner wanted to have his cake and eat it, too. But I can tell you with certainty that many people who have affairs honestly believe these things. Understanding that your partner wanted to protect you rather than hurt you can, over time, help you get past the hurt.

Q: I can't stand being suspicious all the time, but I feel like an idiot for being so trusting in the past. I'm worried that I'll never be able to get over it. Will it ever be the same again? Will I ever really be able to relax and trust?

A: Yes, trust can be restored. But no, it will never be quite the same. Over time—often a long time—trust can once again be strong. The crucial factor in developing trust is the day in and day out sense that you and your partner are making each other feel good. The honest and emotional conversations that many couples have after the discovery of an affair often result in positive changes in the relationship. When the relationship seems better than it was before the affair, trust will slowly but surely develop.

Of course, knowing your spouse had an affair means that you can no longer believe it could never happen. This isn't necessarily a bad thing. All marriages need work to remain vital and gratifying, and the knowledge that things can fall apart can keep you both focused on making your relationship what you want it to be.

Q: It's not fair to focus on what I did to cause him to seek out someone else. He's the one that did something wrong, not me. But we saw a therapist who said we needed to look at my part in what happened. I didn't go back. What do you think?

A: Acknowledging that problems in the relationship partly set the climate for the affair does not mean that you and your spouse have equal responsibility for what happened. However, to go forward you and your spouse need to take a good, hard look at your relationship prior to the affair. Both of you need to understand how each of you has contributed to weakening the relationship. As angry and hurt as you might feel, and as much as you want him to feel remorse for how he has hurt you, focusing on those feelings for too long can be destructive. When one person in a relationship believes that he will forever be the guilty or bad one, despair and anger displace remorse. I've heard many remorseful people say with frustration, "Am I going to have to pay forever? I can't live that way." By acknowledging your share in the problems that existed prior to the affair, you give your spouse some hope that you can eventually work things out between you.

Q: How can I go on in my marriage knowing that my partner was in love with someone else—and maybe still is?

A: Everyone can love someone other than their spouse. When spouses remain faithful to one another, they actively keep themselves from pursuing their attractions to other people. They keep a gate around their heart and though they may peek through it once in a while, they don't ever open the gate completely since love for someone else might easily enter. You, too, could probably fall in love with someone else if you let yourself. So the fact that your partner has fallen in love does not mean that he no longer loves you. If your partner decides that he wants to save your marriage and willingly gives up the other relationship, he will eventually get over his new love. Your partner should have as little contact as possible with the ex-lover. This will enable both of your wounds to heal. Asking him questions about the emotional pain involved in giving up his love will not help you or him. Try your best to let it be.

Q: I hate the idea that my spouse may be staying with me out of convenience. I want him to be with me because he loves me, not because it's the right thing to do, because we have kids, or because it would be financially difficult to separate. I want to know he's with me because he wants to spend his life with me, but how can I believe that when I know he was in love with someone else?

A: There are many types of love. When you have been with someone for a long time, you have shared memories and experiences that contribute to the love you have for each other. The shared love you both have for your children is part of it. The fact that your spouse had a romantic relationship with someone else does not mean that he doesn't love you. As your relationship improves, you will feel your partner's love for you. Some people do stay together for the sake of the children or for financial considerations. But even if that is a primary consideration for staying together, it does not preclude the development of a stronger and more loving relationship than you had before the affair started.

Q: My spouse is annoyed that I need to be reassured of his feelings toward me. He says, "I stayed, didn't I? If I didn't love you, I wouldn't have stayed." But that's just not enough. Am I wrong to keep asking him about his love for me?

A: It can be annoying when someone obsessively asks for reassurance. Your spouse needs to know that in time you will feel better and won't need to ask for reassurance so often. It is also helpful for him to know that compliments and spontaneously expressing warm feelings are far more powerful than the reassurances that you pull out of him.

Seeking Professional Help

If you have tried my suggestions for getting unstuck and you don't notice signs of improvement within a month or two, or if you find that your partner's infidelity has completely devastated and depressed you, you should consider getting professional help. I've heard many people say that although they would go to couples therapy, their spouse would never consider it. Often the reason people don't want to see a counselor is because they expect to hear a lot of criticism and don't see how that will lead to anything but more fighting. But couples therapy is not about mutual accusations and placing blame. It's an opportunity to find out what you *each* are doing that hurts and disappoints the other and to come up with ways to start doing something differently. If you approach your partner with the attitude that you, too, have faults and are willing to learn about *your* role in the marital difficulties, he or she will probably be much more willing to give it a try. Here are examples of the type of statements you might want to make:

- "I'm feeling worried about our marriage, and I'd like to see a marriage counselor to try to make it better."
- "I remember when things were good between us, and I miss those times. If they were good once, why can't they be again?"

- "When I'm mad I blame you for all our problems, even when I know I must be part of them, too. I think a professional could help me see *my* role in this mess!"

When the main upset in your life is your relationship, going to a counselor together is the most appropriate form of therapy. If, however, your spouse refuses to accompany you even after you have presented it in the way just described, then you should consider getting some counseling on your own. The counselor may help you find more effective ways to talk to your spouse. And of course, therapy can help you sort out whether or not you truly want to separate from your partner.

Chapter 7

We Love Each Other, But . . .
Life with Children
Isn't Easy

Most of the couples I counsel love their children deeply. Sometimes it has taken them years of effort to conceive or adopt a child, and most of the first-time parents I see are stunned by the depth of feeling they have for their babies.

Despite the difficulties of parenthood, they feel incredibly lucky and don't wish they could return to being just a couple. Many people feel guilty talking about the negative effect having children has had on their relationship—as if they sound ungrateful. Talking about how your children affect your life also feels dangerous, as if you are tempting fate.

Yet many relationship difficulties are connected one way or another to the stress of the transition from being a couple to being a family. Juggling family life and work isn't easy. With both parents working—as is now the case in the majority of families—couples are stretched to the limit. There isn't enough time for everything and tensions arise over things such as:

- how fairly you divide chores and responsibilities involving the kids.
- time alone versus time as a couple or family.
- the overinvolvement of one parent with the children.

- handling a difficult youngster.
- the loss of romance.
- the effect chronic sleep deprivation has on your sex life.

How to Stay Lovers Even If You Are Parents

The most common dissatisfaction that I hear from couples is that their relationship is more about chores and responsibilities than it is about friendship, intimacy, and fun. When couples become parents they can easily lose the intimacy they had when it was just the two of them. And although you may feel close to one another as parents of a child you both adore, you may find yourself missing the relationship you had before the children came along. Dinners out after work, afternoon jogs, days spent exploring new neighborhoods, weekend camping trips, and the like have been displaced by family outings to the zoo, macaroni-and-cheese, and evenings spent reading *The Tales of Winnie the Pooh*. So often, the warm, cozy family feeling that you dreamed of just isn't there— the kids are cranky, you and your spouse are bickering over chores, and you can't seem to get the baby to sleep. And though you feel deep love for your child and wouldn't trade places with your friends who don't have children, you do wish you and your spouse didn't feel so much like business partners. Romance seems like a distant memory, never to return again.

Stop Feeling Guilty

Many couples feel guilty about wanting to spend time together without their children. The first step in returning to "couple-hood" is understanding that you are not being selfish or neglecting the children if you and your partner spend time together without them. It won't help your children if you feel deprived and stressed. When the lack of time together leads to resentment and tension in the relationship, the children also feel it.

"But with both of us working all week, I hate to leave them with a sitter when I don't have to. I feel guilty. I don't think they see enough of me as it is," says Renee.

Renee's concerns are understandable. It's always difficult to find the right balance between time as a couple and family time, but it's even more difficult when you both work outside the home. Often young children seem taxed to their limits by the amount of time they spend away from their parents. Parents understand this and feel bad about not being able to be there more often for their children. To make up for their time away from the kids, many couples give themselves over almost completely to the children when they are home with them. And this wish to devote themselves to the children isn't just for the kids. Many parents feel upset about the long hours away from their children and miss spending time with them.

But devoting yourself entirely to the needs of the kids when you are home can leave you feeling depleted and deprived. "I look forward to spending time with them, but then I can't wait until they go to bed," says Gerri with embarrassment. Often couples feel guilty because by the end of the weekend they look forward to going back to work. "We try to do a lot of fun things with the kids on the weekends, but all I can say is that the office sure looks good Monday morning," says Diane apologetically.

When you weigh your needs against your child's need for time with you, remember that children are affected not only by time away from their parents but also by the emotional atmosphere of their home. A few more hours away from the children each week will probably matter less in the long run than whether or not you feel close as a couple. In my work with children and families I have frequently noticed how anxious children become when their parents don't get along. Children want their parents to have a good relationship. They may argue when you go out without them. They may ask why they can't sleep in your bed. They may say "It's not fair" that you and Daddy have private conversations. But despite the protests, children feel tremendously comforted by the knowledge that their parents are close; it helps them feel safe and protected. When children know that their parents have a bond between them—separate and apart from their mutual love of the children—they are more comfortable with separations. A child whose parents are having difficulties may worry about sleeping at a friend's house or going to sleep-away camp in fear that the parents can't be close except through him.

Children feel upset when parents aren't getting along, even if they don't always show it directly. Sometimes they misbehave. Sometimes they cry and say they feel scared. Sometimes they get stomachaches. And sometimes they act like the grown-up and try to get their parents to stop fighting. If spending more time away from the children results in a stronger relationship between you and your spouse, the benefits to the children usually make up for the additional hours with baby-sitters.

Tips for Keeping Romance Alive Day In and Day Out

"We need to have a weekend away once in a while. It's been over two years since we spent a night away from the kids. I think if we could take a vacation for a few days a couple of times a year, it would do us a lot of good," says Eileen. Weekends or an occasional vacation without the children can be restorative, but like any vacation, within a few days you fall back in to your old routine. To maintain a sense of yourself as a couple, you need to establish new patterns of behavior, day in and day out. The following tips will show you how to do this in the midst of a hectic life.

Tip #1: Develop a Ritual for You and Your Spouse to Spend Fifteen to Twenty Minutes Alone Together Every Day

Although some couples spend time alone after the children are in bed, by then one or both of you may feel more like having some time to yourself than time together. You will have a little break from the kids if you spend fifteen to twenty minutes with each other when they are awake. If you set firm limits your children will get used to knowing that they can't interrupt during that time.

Many couples say that they have literally no quiet time together at home. They wait until they go out on Saturday night to talk with each other. This happens not only because it's difficult to carve out private time, but also because many couples don't think to do it.

Establishing this time will take self-discipline. It requires not jumping up to do chores, look at mail, make a quick call, or any of the dozens of things that pull on us at home. Think about a time that has a realistic chance of working. Perhaps the kids can take their dessert into another room and you and your spouse can sit at the table for fifteen minutes by yourselves. Or maybe you can have twenty minutes of private time before dinner while the kids play or do their homework. Experiment with what works best for you. It is important to stick to the routine. If done consistently and firmly, your children will soon learn to respect your need for some grown-up time.

The purpose of your time together is to connect with each

other as a couple, not as parents. Therefore it's important to make a concerted effort to talk about things that don't have anything to do with kids and family life. Have the type of conversation you used to have before you became parents. Talk about work, friends, movies, something you read in the paper, office gossip, or chit-chat of any sort, *but try your hardest to leave conversation about kids and responsibilities for another time.*

Tip #2: Go Out Together

Going out can be costly unless you are fortunate enough to have family who will stay with the kids, or friends who will trade off time with you. Even if you can afford a sitter, many people have trouble with the idea of spending so much money to go out to the movies when they can rent a video instead. If you think of this as a date rather than an opportunity to see a particular movie, you may feel better about spending the money. I often tell the couples who see me that baby-sitters are a lot less expensive than marriage counselors and you will help your relationship enormously if you have some time together outside of the house.

Many couples don't want to spend the money to go out because their nights out end up being a disappointment. "Even when we finally do get some time alone, it's not like it used to be," says Gary. "We have to be home early because of the baby-sitter. And when we go out to dinner we always talk about what has to be done, which one of us is going to take care of it, and who is carrying more than his fair share of the load!"

"He's right," says Joanne. "Instead of a date it feels like a planning session. We're both feeling stretched to our limit and when we finally do go out it doesn't feel romantic or intimate."

The experience described by Gary and Joanne is less likely to happen if you follow Tip #1: Make some time every day for nonchildren, nonchore conversation. You will then already have had a lot of experience with rapidly shifting gears from being parents to being a couple. Of course, you need to apply the same rules to your date as you do to your twenty-minute chats—no talking about kids or chores. This may seem difficult to do for an entire dinner. Yet if you can follow this rule it will become a habit and you will feel more like your old selves.

Some people draw a blank when they try to think of some nonchild or nonchore-related topics to talk about. They have trouble accessing the thoughts and feelings that have occurred to them throughout the day. Most of us have had the experience of knowing we have read or heard something interesting and then can't recall it when we finally have a moment to talk about it. Jot things down on a list so that you can refresh your memory when you and your partner have some private time together. The list could include anything from a joke you heard to a feeling you had during a conversation with an elderly aunt. This is particularly useful for people who have trouble talking about their feelings. Writing things down will not only help you recollect them later but will also strengthen your ability to know what you think and feel about things. This may sound contrived, but you will find that your dates will be much more rewarding if you make a conscious effort to engage your spouse in an interesting, nonfamily-oriented discussion.

Tip #3: Have Romantic "Dates" at Home

Dates can also take place at home. Max your special at-home date on your calendar just as if you were getting together with friends. Be strict about not allowing anything to intrude on your plan. Let the answering machine pick up your calls. Make it as much like a real date as possible.

Make sure you do some things that change the atmosphere of the time together so that it will not feel like an ordinary night at home. Plan a special late-night meal to eat after the kids have gone to bed, or put on some soft music and dance. Play cards or a board game. Or plan to spend the evening together in bed. Flowers, notes, and dressing in a special way can create a romantic mood even with the kids asleep in the next room!

Tip #4: Break the Rules

There is something exhilarating about doing things that are not part of your usual routine. Although the need for a baby-sitter makes spontaneous activities difficult, you can break your routine by scheduling baby-sitters for times that you do not usually go out together. Going out during the week rather than only on the weekend can feel like a bit of an adventure. Asking the baby-sitter to stay late once in a while so that you can meet after work for a quick bite can provide a welcome break from the responsibilities of parenthood—and you may find that you feel like a couple of kids playing hooky. You might also want to consider getting a sitter for some daytime hours on the weekend. The point is to do things that will feel like the way it was when you were a couple without children. Again, you must balance the needs of the children against the need to revive your sense of being a couple. If you do this within reason, your children will benefit from the lift in your spirits.

Tip #5: Steal a Sexy Moment

If you feel more like partners running a joint enterprise than lovers, make efforts to remind yourself and each other that sexuality is part of your relationship. Even if you're tired and have difficulty finding a good time to get together sexually, you can remain sexual partners by incorporating a few moments of erotic, sensual touching into your daily life. The stolen sexy caress in the midst of daily life will remind you that you are a couple, not just partners in parenting. If you feel like you've lost interest in sex, or in your partner, don't just accept that feeling. Though it is common to feel a decreased interest in sex when you juggle work and child-rearing, you should not accept it as inevitable. You can do many things to get back to an active sex life with your spouse. See chapter 4 for information about how to help your sexual self come out of hibernation.

Dealing with Your Anxiety About Leaving Your Children with Baby-Sitters

Frequently, one member of a couple complains that they can't pry their partner away from the children. "She's a great mother," says Stan. "I love that she's really there for the kids, and they're crazy about her. But the problem is that she never wants to be away from them. She feels guilty. My brother and sister-in-law have no kids and they're dying to stay with ours for a weekend, but it's always 'Not yet, they're not ready.' I tell you, I'm getting pretty sick of it."

Elliot says, "I'm not her priority anymore. Samantha always comes first. I guess that's the way it should be but I really feel like an outsider. I'm just the guy who brings home the money. They have a great time without me. I don't think I'm important to either of them, really."

And sometimes both partners know that they direct all of their affection and attention toward the children. "I wish he'd give me one tenth of the affection he gives to our daughter," says Dena about her husband. "He's warm and attentive to her every need. I see him with Melissa and I'm jealous of the hugs and kisses he gives her. We used to be more physically affectionate with each other, but now I think we both focus it on her."

It is natural to give your children love and affection, and there is no objective standard for when it is too much or when you are overinvolved. But when one person feels that his spouse's attachment to the children interferes with their relationship, or when one spouse feels excluded, it is important to do something about it. Feeling unimportant may lead your partner to disengage emotionally.

The secure feeling you try to give the children by being there for them can be undermined by the deterioration of the relationship between you and your spouse. Ask yourself honestly if you *do* substitute your child for your spouse, or if you draw the children in around you to the exclusion of your spouse. If the answer is yes, then you need to change your behavior before you seriously damage your marriage.

Often difficulty separating from children has more to do with a parent's anxiety than with the child's upset. "Lucy is a nervous wreck about the kids," says Jack. "She's always afraid something bad is going to happen to them if she's not there. I can hardly ever get her to leave them for a few hours—and overnight is out of the question. I know she really is anxious, but I feel resentful that this gets in the way of our time together."

If you are anything like Lucy, try to challenge and fight your anxiety. The more you give in to it, the worse it will become. If you get reliable and responsible baby-sitters, and gradually extend the time you are away from the children, your fears will diminish naturally. The main thing is that you need to face your anxiety and fight it rather than let it get the better of you. If you cannot overcome your fear with your own efforts, seeking profressional assistance will help your marriage, your children, and yourself.

Resolving Conflicts over Child-Care Responsibilities

"When it was just the two of us, we sometimes argued about who was going to do the cooking or the cleaning and that kind of stuff, but basically it worked out. It wasn't such a big deal. But now Sally always seems resentful. I think I do my share, considering that I work long hours and she only works part-time, but she's mad at me all the time. All we ever talk about is how stressed out she is, and she wants me to admit that I have it easier. I don't get it," says Carl.

Sally responds sarcastically, "You sure *don't*! He doesn't understand how much work is involved in caring for a toddler without any help. The days I go to work are like a vacation compared to the days I'm at home. I think I should go away for a few days and let him see what it's like."

"I leave the house at seven-forty-five every morning and I'm not home until seven at night," says Carl. "And believe me, my job is no picnic! But the minute I walk in she expects me to take over, and most of the time I do. I give Joey a bath and get him ready for bed."

"First of all, most of the time you're home after eight. You *say* you'll be home at seven, but more often then not you end up leaving later than you thought. So most of the time I give Joey his bath. And the days I work, I rush home to pick up Joey from day care and then have to get dinner ready while he wants some attention and needs a bath. You think that just because you give him a bath sometimes and change his diapers, you're Superdad."

"I offer to watch Joey on the weekends so you can go to the gym," says Carl. "And even that offer seems to make you mad. What do you want from me?"

"I get mad because it's like you're *helping out* sometimes as if Joey is really *my* responsibility and you're doing me a favor. You come and go as you please—jogging when you feel like it, going out to do errands, leaving to play golf for half a day. You just tell me what you're doing and assume that I'll be available to be with Joey. What if *I* had made plans?"

"I guess I do act like you're in charge, but I think that's because when I ask you if you want to go somewhere and do something, you act like I wouldn't possibly be able to handle Joey for the day. And when you finally do leave him with me for a few hours, you get upset about what I fed him and what we did. You're like a drill sergeant giving me my orders."

"Well, when you've kept him inside all day because you're watching a football game it makes me mad. Why should Joey be kept in all day just because I go out? This is exactly what I mean. You don't *think*. If I didn't tell you to take him to the park, you wouldn't do it."

"We have a difference of opinion about what he needs. But you think you're the expert. So if that's the way it's going to be, then I think you *should* be in charge. You want me to do things the way you would do them, but I'm a different person."

"It's not fair. I've heard that studies show that women work more hours than men because they go to the office and then they're also responsible when they get home for running a house and bringing up the kids. You play dumb about what to do with Joey and use it as an easy way to get out of your responsibility."

"I don't care what the studies say! Do *you* get the car fixed? Do *you* do the taxes or figure out what kind of pension fund to have? Who filled out the mortgage application?"

"Those things don't compare to what I do and you know it!" Sally says angrily. "You think you don't have to do as much for the family because you earn more money."

"It's *not* the money—you're home a lot more than I am, and I do think you should have more of the responsibility for the home."

"Well, maybe I should go back to work full-time."

"Maybe you should," says Carl angrily.

This argument probably sounds all too familiar. A good deal of bitterness can develop when couples take the positions that Sally and Carl have. As so frequently happens with these types of issues, both of them dig in their heels and feel terribly misunderstood and unappreciated. Instead of listening for the truth in what the other is saying, they look for how they can prove their point. If one of them said something like, "I can sort of see what you mean," rather than answering in some version of "You're wrong," they could make some changes that would create a greater sense of fairness.

Sally and Carl have lapsed into the traditional pattern in which the woman is responsible for home and child-care issues while the husband handles things like finances, cars, and repairs. Even when women work full-time they tend to become the "expert" on child-related issues. And the more they each assume these roles, the more they come to rely on and expect the other to take charge in these areas. Many of the men I work with do indeed play dumb when it comes to things involving the children or homemaking. But often these same men feel quite burdened by having to be the primary wage earner and the one in charge of the finances.

It is natural and efficient to divide up responsibilities. However, you will avoid the type of conflict expressed by Sally and Carl if you each know enough about what the other does to be able to participate in that arena. When Carl stays with the baby, he needs to make a commitment to doing it competently. And similarly, Sally has to learn to deal with car repairs and finances.

If you really want your partner to participate, however, then you must be willing to give up control. Many men complain that their wives micromanage everything related to the kids. "I get interrogated about what he ate, when he napped, how long we were out in the park, and if I used sunscreen," Carl complains. In order to share responsibilities more equally, you must remember that your partner is a separate person whose opinions and ways of doing things differ from yours.

Getting Your Child to Bed Earlier

Difficulty getting children to sleep places an enormous amount of stress on couples. "We play musical beds," says Christopher. "Lynda falls asleep with Ray. He goes to sleep only if she lies down next to him. I wake her up and bring her into our bedroom, but often in the middle of the night Ray wakes up and comes into our bed. Then the baby cries, and even though he goes back to sleep quickly, I can't fall asleep with Ray in our bed so I spend the rest of the night in Ray's bed. I don't know what will happen when the baby gets big enough to come into our bed. It just seems like Lynda and I are never in the same bed at the same time! I know it sounds like I'm joking, but it's a real problem."

I have heard Christopher's story in one form or another over and over again. Many children have learned to rely on having a parent in the room with them, or even lying down with them, in order to fall asleep. It is not unusual for parents to spend an hour, even two, getting a child to bed and then fall asleep themselves next to the youngster. This takes a big toll on time for oneself and as a couple. And to add to the stress, couples feel exhausted when they wake up in the middle of the night or at the break of dawn because their child has not learned how to put himself back to sleep when he wakes up during the night. My experience with

couples and families has shown me that it is enormously beneficial to everybody in the family if children learn to fall asleep
easily in their own room by themselves. Usually it takes no more
than a few days or a week to wean a child from his dependence on
someone else to help him sleep.[4] Those few days will be stressful,
but once your child learns how to do it everyone in the family will
feel much more relaxed. The adults will have more time for
themselves, which will improve their moods, and the children
will get a better night's rest, which will in turn improve their
moods. And as we discussed earlier in the chapter, the happier
you are as a couple, the more secure your children will feel.

Reducing the Stress of Family Life

"I think many of our problems as a couple stem from the fact that
my husband loves the kids but gets so tense when we all spend the
day together," says Lenore. "The kids start fighting, the younger
one has a tantrum because we said no to him, or the oldest
dawdles over his breakfast. Whatever it is, my husband gets mad
and I try to settle the kids down after he's lost his temper with
them. By then I've got a headache. It's so disappointing. We both
work hard all week long, and on the weekends what I thought
would be fun time with them turns into both of us yelling at the
kids and each other. I have a little more patience than my
husband, but I find they really wear me out, too. And I'm worried
that my younger one can pick up on the fact that we are *really*
having a hard time with him. We scold him so much that I'm
afraid of how it will affect him. I don't want him to think that we
don't love him, because we do, but we are both angry at him so
often."

Lenore's disappointment with the time spent as a family is
unfortunately all too common. It's hard to have a good relation-

ship as a couple if time at home is stressful. But some basic principles can help reduce family tensions. These tips come from my work with families and young children and frequently have proven useful in helping both the parents and the children feel more relaxed.

Sometimes Less Is More

Children these days have busy schedules. Often they leave the house early in the morning and return home late in the afternoon. On weekends many kids just don't want to do much. One little girl of seven, who drove her parents crazy with her dawdling and tantrums, said simply, "I don't want to go out on Saturday and Sunday. I have to go to school every day and I just don't want to go out." If you find that your weekends are tense and exhausting, you might experiment with scheduling no activities for one weekend. It may surprise you how relaxed and easy your children become when they don't feel the pressure of having to go somewhere. That doesn't mean you have to let your kids watch TV all day; just don't pack their day with outings. If you set strict limits on TV and videos, they will find other ways to occupy themselves in the long, leisurely hours at home. Many children need to learn how to entertain themselves, and more unstructured time gives them the opportunity to develop this capacity.

Being There When You Are There

It's important to try to protect your family time. Many children I work with wait for hours for one of their parents to arrive home and then misbehave when they have to wait still further while the parent makes "an important call." It's difficult for children not to have access to a parent who is physically present. For many children, especially young ones, phone calls tax the limit of their patience. Try to set aside a certain period of time when you will let your answering machine pick up, and your children know that calls will not interrupt your time with them.

Generally, the more you relax the more the children will relax. Although you already have so little time to get chores done, it can help if you lower your expectations about what you want to accomplish during the weekend. Being relaxed while you are at home with your children is far more important in the long run than completing your chores. Try to finish some of your chores during the week, and only do essential things on the weekend.

Improving Your Child's Behavior

For a variety of reasons, many parents have trouble insisting on good behavior. Sometimes parents felt so squashed as children themselves that they determine to have a more democratic attitude with their own children. These parents worry about "breaking the child's will" and they are committed to not doing to their children what was done to them. Other parents feel so guilty about the time spent away from the children that they hate to say no to them at home. And some parents of very young children with exceptional verbal skills overestimate their child's ability to understand and reason, so they rely on explaining rather than rule setting. If your leniency results in your own resentment and exhaustion after spending time with your child, you are not doing yourself, your marriage, or your child a favor by being nonauthoritarian.

Sam, for instance, makes it clear that he "hates to complain." He and Becky spent five years trying to conceive a child and every time he looks at four-year-old Sara he counts his blessings. "She's great! Boy, did we luck out," he says. "I guess all parents think their kids are brilliant, but she really is special. But being with her is no piece of cake! She's tough. When she wants something, there's no way she'll take no for an answer. By the time we get her down for the night, we're both worn out from all the screaming and arguing."

Seven-year-old Michael kicks, bites, and breaks things when he doesn't get his way. His mother doesn't know what to do. "I know he does it because he's exhausted, but I just can't get him to sleep at night. He wants to see us. We've hardly seen him all day."

Much of my work with families and young children centers on helping parents feel more comfortable setting limits. Tolerating unpleasant and annoying behavior only leads to outbursts and resentment. Upset with a child often leads to an argument with your spouse. Sometimes that occurs because you both feel tired and frustrated, and take it out on one another. Frequently one of you feels the other should have been firmer. Children then feel guilty and worried when parents argue over their behavior. So for the sake of your child, as well as your relationship with your spouse, try to find ways to get children to cooperate.

Time-outs. Time-outs are a highly effective way to help children learn what they can and cannot do. Children feel more secure when they know that their parents will not allow them to behave badly. Set limits as soon as your child starts to act in a way that signals the beginning of trouble to come. Even though you may feel as if you are being excessively firm, it's important to set limits before your child becomes so angry and locked in battle that it's hard for him to calm down and change direction. If you remain firm at a point when nothing too bad has transpired, you will be able to use time-outs more effectively.

Your child may do a number of different things that annoy you. However, tackle no more than one or two problem behaviors at a time. If you come down hard on too many things, your child will feel overwhelmed and won't be able to distinguish what is really important from what isn't.

Time-outs are much more effective when linked with positive reinforcement. You should praise and reward your child with affection when she works hard at being pleasant, easygoing, and cooperative.

Play baby. When children are cranky, whiny, or demanding it affects the whole family. After you have spent many hours trying to cope with a difficult or upset child, you have little emotional energy left over for each other. Many couples have observed that they get along better when their children behave.

In working with difficult children and their parents, I developed a method more than fifteen years ago that still surprises me in how effectively it helps children calm down and get along better with their parents and siblings.

You've probably noticed that your children love looking at pictures and listening to stories about when they were little. Most children look back wistfully on the days when they were younger and less was expected of them. As children grow and mature they like to know that in some way they are still your baby.

When I feel that a child's difficult behavior might be directly related to the stress of growing up, I suggest to parents that they initiate games of Play Baby with their child. Play Baby is a shorthand term covering a wide range of activities, all aimed at reminding the child that no matter how big he gets, or how self-reliant he acts, the parent knows and accepts the youngster's wish to be nurtured as if he were still very young. Parents can initiate pretend games and other activities that cater to the child's baby self. This helps deal with resentments—both expressed and hidden—that an older child may feel for a younger sibling, despite attempts to give the older child equal attention. The parent tells the child that although she is expected to act her age, "You'll always be my baby." Depending on the comfort level of the child and the parent, Play Baby activities can involve anything from wrapping up a school-age child in a "blankie" and giving him a "baba," to reading him a favorite book from his toddler days, to taking out some favorite "baby" toys, to simply reminiscing through stories and pictures about when the child was little.

Play Baby does *not* mean that you relax your standards and expectations. It is not a substitute for limit setting and, in fact, should not be done when your child might interpret it as a reward for misbehavior. If done regularly, you will find that your difficult child becomes much easier and emotionally accessible.

Teaching Your Child to Be Self-Comforting

"Troy has trouble separating from me," says Rebecca about her five-year-old son. "I try not to leave him more than I have to. My husband thinks I'm just caving in and spoiling him. But if we did go out and leave him, I'd worry about how unhappy he was."

"I'm not mad just because I want to go out more often," says Rebecca's husband, Rob. "I know he's scared, but he has to learn to get over it. I'm worried that he'll become a weak, wussy type of kid if we give in to this. Other kids will see him as a crybaby."

The solution to this problem involves giving Troy the skills to cope with separations so that his parents neither cave in nor leave him to sink or swim. The following advice can help conquer separation anxiety in the majority of children.

First of all, children pick up on ambivalence and doubt. When you are absolutely clear and guilt-free about your expectations, children are much more likely to accept separations. If you feel that you are doing a bad thing by going out without your child, he will recognize your hesitancy. Even children who have trouble with separations accept necessary ones, such as when their parents go to work. They have developed coping mechanisms for work-related separations because they receive a guilt-free message from their parents that this is a reality of life they will have to understand. So tell your child, "A baby-sitter is coming over because Daddy and I are going out tonight," and don't ask the child's permission by adding, "Okay?"

Your child needs to develop the capacity to be self-comforting when he is upset. By asking your child what he can do to make *himself* feel better, you communicate that comfort is something that he can give to himself. This reassures the child by making him feel less vulnerable. Your child may be too upset to come up with things by himself that he can do to feel better, but before you make suggestions try to elicit some ideas from him. Many young children love to make lists. You can help your child write down these things or draw pictures that will remind him of things he can do to feel better. The list might include playing video games with the sitter, baking cookies, calling Grandma and Grandpa, or building a fort out of the couch pillows. I have suggested that some parents establish a box of "special" toys for when the child needs something that will really distract him from his anxiety. The child and parent select certain toys that are especially engaging and put them aside for the child to play with when he feels upset and needs self-comforting.

Another important aspect of learning self-comforting behavior is the ability to summon soothing words and thoughts on your own rather than needing to hear them from someone else. When you ask your child what he could say to himself to help him feel better, you give him an important tool to use in many situations throughout his life. Again, your child may need help in coming up with comforting words, but see if he can do it himself before you give any suggestions. These words can range from "I'm okay," "It's safe," "The baby-sitter will take good care of me," "Mommy and Daddy will be here when I wake up," or "Mommy and Daddy love me," to the more complex idea that "Even though I'm mad at Mommy and Daddy, I know they love me."

You might consider using several different sitters—provided that you know they are responsible and caring—in order to help your child recognize that he can have fun with a variety of people. Arranging for the sitter to bring your child an engaging toy for them to play with together once you have left is a tried and true strategy of many parents.

If your child is still crying when you leave, it can help to say something like, "I'm really sorry you're upset, but I bet you and Stacy will come up with some good ideas for having fun when we're gone." Most likely your child will settle down fairly soon after you leave.

Later that night or the next morning, it's helpful to praise your child for having figured out how to make himself feel better. "I'm impressed with you!" you might say. "You were unhappy that we left, but it looks like you did a really good job of finding a way to feel better." The idea is to praise the skill of being self-comforting.

• • •

Often a few sessions with a trained family therapist can help you get on a course that will make family life more pleasant. If you have trouble applying these tips, or have tried but don't see much of a change, you should consider a consultation with a family therapist.

Giving Each Other Some Time Off from Family Life

One of you may desperately need time together as a couple, while the other feels more distressed by the fact that time for individual activities seems to have evaporated.

"My husband feels upset that we don't have much time together anymore," says Karen. "I feel that way, too, but to be honest I'm more bothered by the fact that I never have any time for myself. Between work and the kids, there's nothing left over for me!"

Karen's feeling is a common one. It's not that she doesn't want to spend time with her spouse; she simply feels she doesn't have any breathing space. There's no time for old friends, going to the health club, or doing some leisurely shopping.

Many people long for quiet, private time at home. For some people, time spent alone feels essential to their well-being. Silence, and the opportunity to be alone with their thoughts, can feel as necessary as basic nourishment. So here's an important piece of advice—do not take your partner's wish to be alone as a personal rejection. If, for instance, your partner is the type of person who prefers to jog by himself rather than running with a partner, or likes nothing better than to absorb himself at the computer, space out listening to music, or devour a book, do not interpret this wish to be alone as a wish to be away from you.

The two of you will grow closer as a couple if you try to help one another find the time you each need for yourself. Together, discuss what each of you longs for and how you can best work it out. Often this requires that you each spend more time alone with the children rather than doing things together as a family. Some people have trouble with this because they enjoy the feeling of being together as a group and want their children to have a strong sense of family unity. Life with children requires a constantly shifting balancing act, and time together as a family is certainly an important aspect of what needs to be balanced. But also remember that it's unhealthy for children to watch their parents feel stressed and deprived, and they, too, benefit when their parents feel fulfilled in their own lives.

Chapter 8

We Love Each Other and We Get Along Well, But . . .
Is This It?

Many people I talk to are not sure what to expect from marriage. They know that the early romantic feelings are bound to diminish, but without that life can seem a bit empty. Stable, loving relationships sometimes feel dull. Here are the types of concerns I frequently hear:

- "Is it asking too much to want romance, passion, and good talks after years of being together? Is it enough that we're loyal and there for each other in a crisis? Or that we get along pretty well and are both committed to providing the kids with a stable, secure home?" asks Jayne. *"Is this it?* Is this all that marriage is about?"

- Michelle wearily reports on her weekend. "Alex was worried about something that happened at work on Friday and we talked about it for hours and hours on Saturday and Sunday. I know he was really upset and needed to talk it out and I *want* to be supportive, but *is this it*? Being supportive? Listening to his problems all the time? Is this *marriage*? Sometimes I think it's better to be single. I had more fun when I was single. Listening to problems day in and day out isn't much fun."

- John is committed to his wife, Susie, and has no interest in a divorce, but worries that they don't have much in common anymore. "If we met today, I don't think we'd be interested in each other," he says. "We've gone in different directions in the twelve years since we met. We accept the differences, I guess, but it's kind of a 'live and let live' relationship. If we didn't have kids I think we might consider separating. We don't fight or anything—it's more that we don't get much from each other anymore. I think Susie feels the same way, but we don't talk about it because there's no point. But I guess *this is it*—we are who we are."

- "It depresses me to think that I'll never have romance again. I'm happily married but the romance is gone between us and sometimes I think about having an affair," says Megan. "I know it's stupid, but I really miss romance. Everybody tells me that I'm being unrealistic for feeling so disappointed. But *is this it*? Love without romance for the rest of my life?"

- "I guess long-lasting marriages work because people adjust, get used to each other, and trade excitement for stability," says Lee. "We've been together for almost eighteen years, and I think we're both realists. *This is it.* This is what marriage is about."

- Carla describes a similar concern. "I love my husband and we get along well," she says. "But sometimes I think, *is this it*? Most nights I get home first and fix dinner. Then Dan comes home, we eat, he gets the kids ready for bed while I clean up, we watch a little TV together and go to bed. Saturday we take care of chores, Saturday night we get a sitter and go out, and Sunday we do something as a family. We have sex once a week or so. I know we have a better marriage then a lot of our friends, but it's all so routine. I keep feeling something's wrong with me for wanting more. I'm bored. I love Dan, but he's like an old, comfortable shoe. Am I being childish to think there should be more than this?" she asks.

Therapists are trained not to talk much about themselves. We are there to listen and help people sort out their problems, not to tell them about our lives. We try to stay neutral. We try not to impose our own way on other people. The point is to help couples find what works for them, not to get them to be more like you.

Usually, staying professional and keeping my own life separate from my clients is not hard for me to do. But when I hear them say *"Is this it?"* I find myself wanting to talk about my own marriage, and sometimes I actually do. In fact, I want to shout, "No, no, no—it can be more! Mine is, and yours could be, too. And it's not just luck. It's know-how." This chapter will tell you how to keep your relationship lively and interesting for the rest of your life.

Not in Your Underwear, Please

When I was growing up I heard about a woman who was so concerned about how she looked for her husband that she would put on makeup before she went to sleep at night. This sort of attitude led, in part, to the development of feminism. Thankfully men and women relate to each other more naturally these days. Co-ed dormitories have helped facilitate male-female friendships, and young men and women have a comfort and lack of pretense with each other that is by and large very positive.

But sometimes feeling comfortable with each other goes too

far. When I say "Not in your underwear, please," I don't just mean what you wear in front of one another, although that *is* part of it. I am talking more generally about an attitude many people have that they shouldn't have to do anything to stay attractive to their spouses, both physically and otherwise. Some couples relate to one another with little regard for politeness or manners. These couples assume that they shouldn't have to make any effort to be appealing or interesting to their partners. Instead they are "natural" with one another—perhaps the way they were with their siblings when they were growing up. They don't worry about how they look or act. They will burp or pass gas unselfconsciously because they don't think of their partners as people with whom they need to have good manners.

I've heard many people say that they aren't interested in having sex because their partners don't shower often enough, have bad breath, or go to sleep in a dirty, ripped T-shirt or sweat suit. These concerns should be taken seriously. They are not just excuses, as some people think. They have a real effect on sexual desire and they encourage your partner to think of you as an old friend, not a lover.

So an absolutely basic component of keeping a serious relationship romantic is always to be aware of the need to stay attractive to your partner. I'm not talking about the occasional time you wear a sexy negligee to bed. I'm referring to the way you act and look day in and day out, year after year. Lounging around in your nightgown all day rather than getting dressed, or wearing sloppy dirty clothes, because you are home and want to be comfortable is not conducive to romance. Remember that if you want your partner to remain a lover, comfort with each other must have its limits.

The Problem with Doing What Comes Naturally

Many couples think that they shouldn't have to concern themselves with being polite when they are at home. "Home is the place where I want to be able to put my business self on the shelf," says James. "All day I've been careful about what I say and how I act. When I get home it's a relief to be myself." Of course James is right. We all want and need a place where we can let down our guard. We want our home and our intimate relationship to be this safe haven. The problem is that when you do what is natural, you sometimes act in ways that contribute to the loss of romance in your relationship. Many couples are shocked when I tell them this. By politeness I do not mean simply saying "Thank you" and "Please," although these words and the attitude that goes with them certainly help. I mean making some effort to treat your spouse with the same courtesy you would give to a friend or even an acquaintance.

Couples behave impolitely when they stop thinking of their spouse as someone they need to relate to in a consciously sociable manner. For instance, when Joe comes home and his wife, Carol, doesn't get off the phone soon after, her impolite behavior suggests that he is not important to her. And when John looks at his mail at the dinner table, or gets up to do something while his wife is still eating, he is taking her for granted and communicates that she is unimportant. Couples who go to bed at different times need to say good night to one another and not simply disappear. The same applies to entering or leaving the home—a social greeting will let the other person know they are more than a piece of furniture in the house! Saying routine phrases such as "Good morning," "How did you sleep?" and "How was your day?" communicates that no matter how well you know each other and think you might know the answers, you are still interested.

When you add what I call *tender gestures of caring* to traditional politeness, you strongly enhance the feelings of warmth and love that exist between you and your partner. Extending your hand to help your partner out of a taxi, offering to carry something if her hands are full, helping him put his coat on, unlocking her car door before your own, guiding him through a crowd, offering your jacket if your partner is chilled, and dropping your partner off at the door before parking the car are all gestures that say you care about your partner. These gestures, by the way, need to go in both directions. Both sexes appreciate being helped on with their coat or unburdened of one of their packages.

How Not to Become an Old Shoe

• When Mary comes home from work she almost always launches into a description of the trials and tribulations of working for an inconsiderate and overly demanding boss. She's wound up. She's tense. And she looks forward to unburdening herself to her husband. She goes into a detailed description of the annoying events at her office and after about half an hour she feels better. Her husband, Timothy, loves her and he's sorry that she's in a job she doesn't like. He has learned to suppress his wish to solve her problems, and instead he tries hard to listen sympathetically. But he is bored and worn out from the same old "conversation." I use quotes because, in fact, Timothy and Mary are not really having a conversation. He is being a dutiful husband and listening to Mary attentively, but he has heard the same thing many times and patiently waits until he can return to the program he was watching. They've been away from each other all day, but Timothy has little desire to spend time with his wife in the evening. It's not that he doesn't love her. It's simply that she doesn't talk about things that hold his interest, and he'd rather watch TV or read a book than listen to her talk obsessively about the things that are bothering her.

- Sally and Frank both work in the city. They drive home together when they can coordinate it, but Sally often wishes during the drive that she were sitting by herself on the train. It's not that she doesn't love Frank, but driving home with him isn't enjoyable. He's always angry and seething at the "assholes" in the other cars. She knows that he's just tense from work and letting off steam, but she hates being around him when he's like this. It makes her anxious, and instead of enjoying the time together without the kids she just closes her eyes and tries to ignore him.

- "My husband, Lenny, has no patience for incompetence," says Louise. "I agree with him. But he's so bothered about it that when it's happening he becomes preoccupied and can't let it go. Often when we go out to eat I wish we had stayed home. It's hard to have a good conversation with someone who is distracted and mad about the bad service in the restaurant. I wish he could just let it go, but I guess he can't. He hates being passive when something is wrong and I basically respect him for that attitude. But it's like he's not really there once he gets mad at something, and I never know when it's going to happen."

Frank, Mary, and Lenny all feel that marriage means being able to let go and act the way you feel. And, in fact, their spouses share this assumption and try hard to tolerate their bad moods. But when you chronically unburden yourself to your spouse, though your partner may accept your behavior it can lead to emotional distancing.

Timothy says that he often prefers to go out for a drink with a friend before coming home. He hopes that if he comes home later, Mary will already have calmed down a bit and he won't have to endure so much complaining. Louise guiltily confesses that she would rather go out with other couples than be alone with Lenny because he doesn't let himself get as worked up. "I guess with me he can just be himself. But to be honest I like him better when he's around other people. He just doesn't let things bother him as much, and when he relaxes he's great." Alice realizes that sometimes she takes on more work than she should because if she leaves a little later she takes the train home instead of driving with Frank.

Over time, the little wedge that exists between these couples can and usually does become bigger and bigger. Mary, Frank, and Lenny never think about whether or not their behavior is appealing to their spouse. In order to preserve the vitality of a relationship over the long haul you must continue day in and day out to care about being engaging and interesting to your partner. When you stop caring about that, you set the stage for a serious deterioration of your relationship.

Of course, an important component of love is the willingness to be there for your partner and to hear him out when he is upset. When people feel stressed, angry, frustrated, insecure, uncertain, or sad, they want to talk about their anxieties to their partner. Sometimes people simply have to get something off their chest or talk it out over and over again until they feel better. Please understand that I'm not suggesting that you pretend to feel okay when you're not, but I am suggesting that chronic and constant expression of negative feelings can wear thin the patience of even those who love you the most. It is important to remember that your "real" self is as much how you act with friends as it is how you act when you make little or no effort to be interesting. If your partner loves you and feels committed to you but doesn't enjoy time spent with you he may begin to have that "Is this it?" feeling.

How to Stay Interested in Each Other for the Rest of Your Lives

When I was in my late teens I often wondered what it would be like to be married. Could two people really stay interested in one another for thirty, forty, or fifty-plus years? It seemed almost impossible. Wouldn't you know everything about one another after a while? What could you possibly talk about if you spent every day of your lives together? Today, after more than thirty years of marriage, I sometimes step back and shake my head in amazement that my husband and I continue to find each other interesting. So I understand the question that I hear often—how can you be with the same person year in and year out, day after day after day, and not get bored? I've given a lot of thought to that question and here's the answer I've come up with: My husband and I have not been married to the same person all these years. Of course I do not mean that we have had secret lives or marriages! But we each have changed and become different in many ways over the years. Neither of us is the same person that we were when we first met and married.

Encouraging and Noticing Change

One of the secrets to a successful long-haul marriage is that you each allow, support, notice, and appreciate the ways the other is changing. Often people have affairs because the lover sees and values aspects of them that their spouse doesn't notice. When, for instance, you are the serious and responsible one in your marriage, it feels great to be seen by your lover as playful and a bit wild. Or if your spouse thinks of you as unemotional, it is almost irresistible to have someone respond to you as a "feeling" person.

If you think about it, we sometimes behave differently with certain people. We all have many possible selves. Different people bring out different aspects of our personalities, and when this other self receives a positive response it tends to get stronger and stronger.

Many people feel different at work from who they are at home and wish that their spouse knew them the way their coworkers do. You may feel that your spouse doesn't show much empathy when you're upset, yet at work people may think of him as an encouraging and supportive manager. Or you may feel that your spouse is passive when it comes to making decisions, yet her boss may compliment her for her "take-charge" style.

There are two reasons why we don't see certain traits in our spouses that other people do see. First, we humans seem to have our brains wired in such a way that we often see what we expect to see rather than what is actually there. If you know, for instance, that your spouse is not very good at expressing emotions, you will have a hard time noticing when he actually does express his feelings well. If your spouse thinks of you as an extravagant spender, he is not likely to register it when you go bargain-hunting.

The second and related reason that spouses often don't know certain aspects of each other is that they actually do act differently at home. There are many reasons for this, but a simple one is that we tend to get into certain patterns with people and when our new behavior isn't noticed or responded to positively, we quickly return to a more familiar way of acting. Like it or not, good or bad, we all tend to live up to others' expectations of us. Just as we want our parents to see us for who we are now as adults, most of us also want our spouses' view to keep pace with who we have become. You will strengthen the love between you and make your marriage much more interesting if you notice and applaud the changes in each of you.

Giving up your monopoly. A big part of allowing your partner to grow and change involves giving up your monopoly on particular personality traits. Often couples have rigid definitions of themselves and of each other. "I'm the sociable one and he's the loner," "I'm aggressive and she lets anybody roll right over her," or "I'm emotional and he doesn't let his feelings out" are the type of statements that most couples make. Interestingly, even when couples disagree about a lot of things, they generally don't disagree about these descriptions of themselves or their spouses. In the hundreds and hundreds of couples I have worked with, I can't think of a time when one person said, "No, that's not true— I *do* express emotions," or "I *am* sociable." Couples tend to define themselves in comparison to each other, and this, unfortunately, is part of why many people find it hard to grow, change, and evolve with their spouse.

Supporting change in your partner means letting go of these definitions and roles. If you can accept, for instance, that both you and your spouse can be sociable, emotionally expressive, or assertive, many more options are open to both of you. When you have rigidly defined roles each person remains stuck for life in a role that they may no longer want to have. By noticing and supporting "out-of-role" behaviors, you and your partner give each other one of the most valuable gifts possible—the gift of being really known. Your spouse will feel loved and appreciated if you notice that he seems more able to hold his own with his highly competitive brother, is calmer about dealing with his difficult boss, comes across as more relaxed socially, is more organized, is becoming more self-confident when he gives presentations, or doesn't seem as anxious about business trips. There is an intimacy in observations of this sort that comes with having known each other for a long time.

Becoming Someone New

As I said earlier, my husband and I are not the same people we were when we met and married. I was a shy, young law student who found being called on in class agonizing, and today I am a psychologist who comfortably speaks to audiences of two thousand people. And although my husband did not change careers the way I did, the breadth of his interests and his way of being in the world changed dramatically over the lifetime we have spent together. One of the wonderful things about being in a stable relationship is that it frees up emotional energy that can be used to grow and change. When you no longer have to worry about whether you will meet the right person, cope with hurt feelings and rejections, deal with the uncertainty about his feelings for you or yours for him, or try to decide whether your relationship warrants a stronger commitment, you have more time and emotional energy. I remember having a strong sense of freedom from these concerns once the stress and strain of the early years in my marriage were largely straightened out. Hours that had been spent arguing, apologizing, and sorting out differing expectations could now be devoted to other things.

If you are in a stable, loving relationship, the best thing that you can do to keep it lively is to continue to develop and change throughout your life. Perhaps the most important piece of advice in this whole book is this: *Never say, "This is the way I am," or "This is what I like or don't like."* By this I mean don't pigeonhole yourself. Do you remember when you were a child and your mother urged you to try new foods? Well, she was right. You owe it to yourself to at least try things before you decide that they really aren't for you. Many women who grew up thinking "I'm not interested in sports" or "I'm not athletic" have discovered as adults that they get tremendous pleasure from athletic pursuits. People who never sang because they couldn't carry a tune have, as adults, learned to play a musical instrument. People who believed they couldn't draw a straight line to save themselves have become passionate about art. People who dreaded language class in high school have been amazed that through language immersion programs they learned to speak a foreign language. You will find your life and your marriage much more interesting if you remain open to trying new things and having new experiences. It may sound paradoxical, but the more fulfilled you are on your own, the more fulfilling you will find your marriage. If you engage in activities you like to do, you will bring home with you joy, energy, enthusiasm, interesting stories, and experiences. These good moods are often contagious. It's not easy to juggle a job and children, but even a little time spent developing your own interests is time well spent. When you focus on your interests— rather than on what your spouse is or is not giving you—you will take the pressure off of the relationship. The fuller your life becomes, the less you will look to your relationship to fill a void—an expectation that is inevitably disappointing. No matter how much your partner loves you, love alone cannot make life interesting.

Growing Together, Not Apart

Life is a balancing act, and figuring out how to "do it all" in the face of limited time is a never-ending problem. The more things you enjoy doing, the more balls you have to keep in the air. So, at the same time that you develop and grow as an individual, you need to make sure that you and your spouse also grow together.

When you and your spouse first started out, you probably talked about the things you would do together one day. Perhaps you imagined yourself building a ski house, driving cross-country, having a family band with your kids, or going on long wilderness adventures. Hopefully you have actually done some of the things you dreamed of when you first met. Doing things together, or even the dreaming of the things you would like to do someday when you have fewer parental responsibilities, keep you close even as you each evolve and change as individuals. You will find that as different as you think you and your spouse have become over the years, you can do a lot of these things together if you each remain open to new experiences. When your spouse thinks of something he'd like to do together—camping, golfing, deep-sea fishing, learning a language, taking a course, refinishing old furniture—be inclined to say, "Okay, I'll give it a try." Joining in each other's activities and fantasies is one of the most important ways that you can keep romance alive for the rest of your lives.

The Imposter Game

I don't remember exactly how it started, but one day years ago my husband and I started playing what we call "the imposter game." Here's how it goes: Suppose a Martian abducted your spouse, and the Martian—who could make himself look exactly like any person he abducted—returned to Earth impersonating your spouse. In preparation, the Martian found every bit of information he possibly could about your spouse from everyone who knows him *except* you. What do you know about the habits and thoughts of your spouse that no one but you (and maybe your children—if you want to add that to the game) knows? What mistakes would the Martian make that would let you know that the person sharing your life and your bedroom was not really your spouse? For instance, are you the only one who knows that your spouse sings in the shower, is afraid of okra, or has a ticklish spot that you can torture him with if you're in a mischievous mood? Or, on a more serious note, do you know something about his reactions in a crisis that no one but you would know? Or what he's like when he's worried or sick? Or a nightmare that he has had repeatedly? We continually add new items to the list of things the imposter would never know, and when one of us does something a little quirky we'll often point out to each other, "That's one for the imposter game."

I'm telling you about this game because I think it captures some of the pleasure of familiarity and intimacy. But part of the delight of this pastime is that we can always add to our list of what only the other knows. We add to the list precisely because we each continually change and surprise one another.

Even though we have been to hundreds of movies together since we met, we often sit silently through a movie wondering whether the other might actually like this awful film! Knowing each other well, we can usually make an accurate prediction, but many times we are shocked by our partner's reaction. And though we may feel horrified that our spouse liked something that we thought was awful, we always enjoy the fact that we're still somewhat unpredictable.

So I will end this book with one more tip:

Continue to Surprise Yourself and Your Spouse

We all know that little surprises can enhance romance. Buying flowers, gifts, or champagne, or leaving a love note or a sexy message on the answering machine reminds your spouse that you still think of him romantically. Romantic gestures of this sort are wonderful, and usually the more you give the more you will receive.

But surprising yourself and your spouse can mean much more than that. Have an "I'm game" attitude and a willingness to try new things. Have little adventures together and apart. Take up a new hobby or learn a sport you thought you could never do. Start to tell jokes. Take up swing dancing, playing the banjo, or learning to cook Chinese food. Meet your spouse for a drink after work, go hear some jazz, or play pool together.

Start acting in ways that your spouse doesn't expect. Join your spouse in his interests when he assumes that you won't. I remember the delighted and shocked look on my husband's face when I, who never watched basketball, started reading about the Knicks so that my husband could have someone to talk to about his obsession. Although it was hard to sustain—I learned the names of the players and even got into the talk about trades, but I just didn't enjoy actually watching the games—I think my husband was touched by my effort to be a pal. And when he surprised me by agreeing to learn to dance to Cajun music because I thought it might be fun, I knew we'd be lovers for life!

The mix of old and new—familiarity and surprise—makes long marriages possible and wonderful. I hope this book will help you and your partner keep the spark and passion alive forever and ever.

Appendix
A Note for Couples Therapists on How to Help Couples Follow the Tips in This Book

The ideas in this book come directly from my work as a couples therapist. Many colleagues who read an early version of this book felt that its tips would be very helpful to the couples they work with, but were concerned that they are easier said than done. "These suggestions sound great on paper," I've been told, "but how on earth can I ever get the couples I work with to follow them when they are so defensive and blaming of one another? And what about resistance? How do you deal with the resistance to change that seems to be part of the makeup of so many people?"

These are valid concerns. Often, one person in the couple is reluctant—to say the least!—to act differently, and the best advice in the world is worthless if it isn't followed. So in keeping with the practical approach of this book, this brief note offers therapists some concrete suggestions for how to increase the motivation of resistant clients.

Of course, these suggestions won't work with everyone. But I have found that *most* people who seek couples counseling (even those who are essentially brought to therapy by their spouses) really want things to be better between them and can often, though not always, learn to be open, nondefensive, and receptive to suggestions.

Being a couples therapist is hard work. The most seasoned therapists sometimes feel daunted by their mission: to turn arguments into productive discussions in which each person's hurts, needs, wishes, and disappointments are not only heard but also empathized with by his or her partner. An occupational hazard of being a couples therapist is that we are in danger of absorbing the couples' sense of hopelessness and may become despairing ourselves about the possibility of change taking place. Negative feelings are often contagious, and without some concerted effort on our part we may find ourselves primarily in the role of the one who points out problems rather than offering solutions.

Noticing Positives

There are two reasons why it helps to notice positives in a relationship when at all possible. First, reluctant participants in couples therapy often feel that their spouses are exaggerating the marital problems and seeing the glass as half empty rather than half full. When the therapist indicates that she sees strengths in the relationship, the resistant partner feels affirmed and begins to have more trust in the process. Second, in order to agree to try something new, clients need to feel that their relationship isn't hopeless. Often, one or both of them feels pessimistic about *anything* helping. To counteract this despair, I help couples see what is still good in their relationship despite all of their difficulties.

In a first session, after hearing about the problems that have led them to seek counseling I ask the couple to reflect on what goes well in their relationship despite the serious problems that have led them to seek help. Are they good parents? Do they work well on big projects, such as renovating a house? Are they good together in a crisis? Do they get along well with each other's families? Do they enjoy entertaining together, creating a warm atmosphere for guests? Do they give each other helpful input about work? Do they have fun on vacations? This simple line of questioning begins to instill some hope. Many people expect therapy to be about complaints, criticisms, and counterattacks, with a third person acting as referee. Knowing that we will look for and build on strengths reassures couples who may fear that going to therapy will do nothing but open a can of worms.

You can also instill optimism by training yourself to notice and comment upon the positive interactions between the couple. Often these go unnoticed because the problems and negative interactions dominate everyone's psyche. Does the couple listen attentively to one another without interrupting, even though they may disagree? Do they sometimes answer nondefensively rather than just counterattacking? Is there an occasional smile or laugh in the midst of the discussion of difficulties? Couples often feel so demoralized by their negative interactions that they lose sight of the positives that remain.

Noticing positives in a relationship can be thought of as a type of compliment. If compliments are to be effective, they must be genuine; otherwise they will be seen as nothing more than patronizing manipulations. The more *specific* the positive feedback, the more believable and powerful it will be.

An important caveat about noticing positives: The couple will only feel more hopeful if they know that you see the positives in the context of understanding the seriousness of their difficulties. If you don't convey a real understanding of the intensity of their negative interactions, they will think that your comments on positive interactions are nothing more than trying to sweep their problems under the rug.

Setting Priorities

Effective work with couples requires that the therapist help the couple set priorities. It is important to sort out the hodgepodge of dissatisfactions that couples come in with into circumscribed and clearly delineated difficulties. Too often couples link serious concerns and minor difficulties together and this piling on of complaints leads one member of the couple to feel hopeless and angry. "Nothing I do is right" is an all-too-familiar refrain to couples therapists. To counteract this feeling, it is important not only to note the positives in the interaction, but also to help the couple decide together what problems they should tackle first. By defining specific problems and working on only one or two issues at a time, the therapist can help the couple feel less overwhelmed and give them a sense of accomplishment as they gradually make progress. In general, try to start with the issues that seem most amenable to change. Success breeds success, and as the couple experiences their relationship improving even in small ways, it encourages and motivates them to work on more difficult problems.

Conveying to the couple that there are specific ways to work on clearly defined issues helps them feel more hopeful. When you have a plan of action and specific things that can done about a problem, it looms less large. Often couples (and therapists as well) have difficulty translating understanding into action. You can use specific chapters in this book to generate ideas for what to do about the problems once you have clearly defined them.

Individualizing the Suggestions in This Book

Every couple and every individual is unique. No book can take the place of the specific understanding and shaping of suggestions that takes place in couples counseling. What works for one couple may be useless for another, even when solving the same type of problem. Couples counselors bring an understanding of the effect of family background and individual psychodynamic issues to the difficulties the couple is encountering. When using the suggestions in this book, the couples therapist can help modify them so they more accurately fit with the particular issues at play.

Couples are more likely to follow through on the tips in these chapters if the therapist helps each person to express reservations, concerns, and hesitancies about the ideas offered. Once both partners agree upon a plan of action, it helps to brainstorm together about the difficulties they might encounter when they try various problem-solving strategies. When the couple experiments with new ways of interacting, it's important to help them be realistic about what to expect from their first attempts at trying something new. Often couples can't spontaneously see the progress they are making and need the therapist to highlight and notice changes when they occur. And of course, not infrequently couples will try something new and get disappointed when they find themselves in a major disagreement or argument.

Perhaps the most important task of the therapist is to help the couple get back on track when some attempt at new behavior has not gone well—helping them change direction rather than give up entirely when a "solution" fails to work. Clients can easily feel demoralized, and it is important to make sure that they don't feel blamed for the suggestion not working. If you share the responsibility and convey that *together* you had not sufficiently anticipated potential problems you will often motivate the couple to try again in a different way.

Strengthening Motivation

A rule of thumb in doing the sort of couples therapy that motivates clients to try new behaviors is that whenever a choice has to be made regarding what part of a comment to address, it is generally best to respond first to what is going *well* rather than what is going *wrong*. Prefacing a focus on the problems with statements that underline instances of openness and goodwill increases motivation and leads to more positive efforts. Noticing, for instance, that a person is "trying hard to understand your partner's point of view" or "asking questions that indicate a real willingness to take in what is being said" reinforces important steps in the right direction. Thus, if a generally closed and defensive person admits in a session to some unconscious motivation, such as "Well, maybe I was angrier than I realized," or "I guess what I did was a bit provocative," the therapist, before going further into the issue, should *first* note the candor and openness with which he or she is speaking. This in itself is likely to lead to more openness.

Even when a couple argues in a session, it's important to attend to any *positives* in the way they are arguing. One might notice aloud that although they are very angry at one another, they are doing well in maintaining control, or are not hitting below the belt, or are not engaging in character assassinations. When this type of positive observation precedes a discussion of the argument, you are likely to get more cooperation in looking for solutions than when you focus only on the argument itself.

Another way to increase cooperation and willingness to try these tips is through the use of *positive attribution*. This involves noticing the slightest bit of motivation and attributing to the couple or the individual the wish to act differently. Thus for example, if the wife sighs and says, "I really do have a bad temper," the therapist might comment on the fact that she seems disturbed by this and would like to do something about it. Attributing positive motivation to a client, even when he or she may not yet be aware of any such motivation, can be helpful. By articulating a yet unformed wish to change, the therapist in fact encourages moves in a productive direction. Similarly, when some change has already occurred, it helps to attribute these changes not to chance, but rather to a desire on the part of the couple to find solutions to their problems. For instance, in saying something like "I'm struck by how you seem to want to resolve your differences, because today you are really listening to your wife, even though you still disagree with her," you amplify a desire and effort to make things better of which the patient himself may have only been slightly aware.

In order for attributions to be effective, they must resonate with some aspect of the individual's experience. There has to be a core of validity to what is being said. Attributions tap into one side of a person's confused and often contradictory feelings. An angry spouse, for instance, may want to stay angry and yet at the same time want to let go of the anger. When the therapist underlines actions and statements that indicate the latter, it actually gives strength to the positive side of the person's ambivalence. There is some element of suggestion here, but it only "takes" if it makes sense to the client.

It is beyond the scope of this appendix to go into the complex nuances of effective therapeutic communication with couples. For helpful, concrete suggestions on how to talk to clients in ways that facilitate listening, I suggest you read Paul Wachtel's *Therapeutic Communication: Knowing What to Say When* (New York: Guilford Press, 1993).

● ● ●

Love, sexuality, empathy, and fun can and often do return when couples actively try to substitute new actions for old patterns. I hope this book will enable you to better translate complex understandings into doable behaviors. The most important thing you can offer couples is your conviction that new behavior can and does lead to new ways of feeling. The suggestions in this book will help you get your clients to alter problematic interactions so that empathy, love, and commitment can resurface.

Notes

[1]National Center for Health Statistics, *Final Divorce Statistics*, March 22, 1995.

[2]Abigail Trafford, "Romance Expectancy on the Rise," *The Washington Post*, July 22, 1997.

[3]Preston, E.M. *The Temper Tantrum Book.* (1969) Viking: New York.

[4]See Richard Ferber, *Solving Your Child's Sleep Problems*, (1985), for advice on helping your child fall asleep by himself.

Acknowledgments

I want to thank my agent, James A. Levine, for his enthusiastic response to this project; my editors, Cassie Jones and Lara Asher, for the care they took in going over the manuscript; and Robert Asahina, president and publisher of Golden Books Adult Publishing Group, for his invaluable help in conceptualizing and shaping the presentation of the material.

I also want to thank the hundreds of couples whose openness and trust have taught me so much, and who have given me the gift of letting me help them strengthen and maintain their love.

About the Author

Dr. Ellen Wachtel, author of two highly influential books for professional therapists, is widely known in the field of marriage and family therapy. She has a Ph.D. in psychology and a law degree from Harvard Law School. She has taught at the Ackerman Institute for Family Therapy, New York University, the City University of New York, and New York City's St. Luke's-Roosevelt Hospital. Married for more than thirty years and the mother of two grown children, she lives in New York City.